My Morning Cup

My Morning Cup

And Other Spiritual Thoughts

Jeanie Shaw

ILLUMINATION
PUBLISHERS

www.ipibooks.com

My Morning Cup
©2023 by Illumination Publishers International

Printed in the United States of America

Cover Design: Toney C. Mulhollan
Interior Design: Thais Gloor

ISBN: 978-1-95872391-3

To my children and grandchildren—
the most wonderful pressed down, heaped up,
running over and "sitting on my lap" blessings
I could ever imagine.
I pray that your cups (be they mugs or sippy cups)
will always be held out before God
to be filled, poured out and refilled to overflowing.

Contents

Other Writings

Wisdom for Life

In the Wisdom for Life devotional series, older women with years of life experience and biblical insight share truths that have helped them and others through the years.

If you sometimes wish you could just sit down at the table across from a spiritual mom and hear some of the important things she has learned in her life, this is your chance.

Gloria Baird wrote the first volume, entitled *God's Pitcher*; Sheila Jones wrote the second volume, *My Bucket of Sand*; and Linda Brumley wrote the third volume, *My Beggar's Purse*. In this fourth volume by Jeanie Shaw, *My Morning Cup*, you will hear some stories of amazing happenings in her life...along with some spiritual lessons she has learned from them all.

Each volume will be unique because each woman, like you, is one of a kind.

We pray that as you read, you will be encouraged and will gain "wisdom for life."

Likewise, teach the older women to be reverent in the way they live, not to be slanderers or addicted to much wine, but to teach what is good. Then they can train the younger women to love their husbands and children, to be self-controlled and pure, to be busy at home, to be kind, and to be subject to their husbands, so that no one will malign the word of God. (Titus 2:3–5)

My Morning Cup of Learning

What's in your morning cup?

As a New Englander I cherish my morning cup of coffee. I love going to my corner chair, throwing a lightweight blanket over my lap and reading my Bible while sipping the delectable brew. At one time coffee seemed bitter and was of no interest to me. Besides, my mother once told me I was too young to drink it.

One day, when I was in my early forties, it occurred to me that I was probably old enough to try this once forbidden beverage. I carefully brewed a pot, and the rest is history. I was hooked!

I like it steaming hot, decaffeinated and with cream only (no milk please!). A mug is best; certainly no Styrofoam container is worthy to surround this smooth, creamy brown java treat. I enjoy it morning after morning and never tire of the taste.

As I fill my cup with coffee, I also allow God to fill my spiritual cup with his truth and guidance. Although I am careful not to pour my coffee to overflowing, God is not as "careful." I find that my cup from God overflows on a daily basis. His word fills my heart to the brim and more. His love is never-ending, bottomless. His wisdom is rich and deep. The strength of his power is more than I can grasp.

Over the years Isaiah 50:4 has become a treasured scripture to me. I have it displayed in a small frame, resting on the windowsill above my kitchen sink:

> The Sovereign Lord has given me an instructed
> tongue,
> to know the word that sustains the weary.
> He wakens me morning by morning,
> wakens my ear to listen like one being
> taught.

What a vivid, amazing description the prophet Isaiah portrays of awakening morning by morning with an eagerness to listen and be taught. Is this how you awaken each day—holding your cup up to God and allowing him to fill it with that love, wisdom and mighty strength? Are you eager for God to "top off" your morning cup from him?

I want to daily "listen like one being taught" by God. I want to drink from that bottomless cup.

Jesus was the master at noticing life around him and using object lessons to teach his disciples spiritual truths to apply to their lives. He implanted the Scriptures so deeply into his heart that we see them come quickly as he faces intense temptation in the desert. As a boy he is found asking questions of the elders in the temple. We get a glimpse of lessons he has learned about human nature as he asks a crowd who would like to "throw the first stone."

Insights derived from physical nature flow from him as he recounts lessons learned from lilies of the field. He was careful to communicate exactly what the Father wanted him to say and how he wanted him to say it! We are also told he learned obedience through the challenges that he suffered.

If Jesus, the perfect son of God, so readied himself as a learner, how much more must I have an eagerness to learn!

Learning is a funny thing for me. Sometimes it's accidental, but most often it's purposeful. If I don't set my mind and heart to be attentive to God, I can certainly fall into the trap of going through a day unaware of what I can learn.

I believe we can all make progress in learning "on purpose" how to apply God's word to our everyday lives. If we don't listen to and learn these lessons from the truth of God, we can be traveling in a dizzying maze that leads us nowhere and leaves us ill-prepared to cope with what yesterday brought, today has in store and tomorrow will bring.

The more familiar we become with the Scriptures, the more apt we are to use them; and use them we must! It is not enough for them to just be familiar to us. While we certainly need to read them, study them and hear them taught and preached in order to internalize them, it is imperative that we also meditate on them in the quiet of our minds, write them on our hearts through memory and repetition, and put them into practice.

Scriptures are to be used in our daily walk when times are both mundane and extraordinary! We need to exercise them in our thought patterns—whether problem solving or day dreaming. We must use them in our conversations with those close to us and others we encounter. This is how we learn!

What if we approached every situation, every relationship, every worship service, every conversation and every new day with an attitude of learning and "being taught"? Would we not more likely gain healthy growth instead of hurtful bitterness and criticalness? Would we not be more apt to see life in a more faith-filled way?

And what are we to do with the lessons we learn? Should we just internalize them so we can be stronger, wiser individuals? What good are lessons learned if we don't use them and share them? They would be of no benefit to anyone and would just tempt us with pride. Learning is not meant to cause us to be arrogant, but to help us grow ourselves and share with others. As Isaiah states, drawing back from God's lessons would be rebellious:

> The Sovereign Lord has opened my ears,
>   and I have not been rebellious;
>   I have not drawn back. (Isaiah 50:5)

I anticipate my morning cup of learning and I desperately need it. I don't want to refuse this cup.

Most of the chapters are set up in two parts: (1) recounting an experience I have had and (2) sharing what my cup of learning is from that experience. The coffee cup symbol will be your signal that the "cup of learning" part is coming up.

My prayer is that you and I will drink together from our morning cups with a renewed zeal to apply the Scriptures to our daily lives, thus molding the way we think and live…morning by morning.

When Your Pages Are Misnumbered

> Peter turned and saw that the disciple whom Jesus loved was following them. (This was the one who had leaned back against Jesus at the supper and had said, "Lord, who is going to betray you?") When Peter saw him, he asked, "Lord, what about him?"
>
> Jesus answered, "If I want him to remain alive until I return, what is that to you? You must follow me."
>
> John 21:20–22

The package arrived in the mail, and I was eager to dig into the new book, *My Bucket of Sand*, by my friend Sheila Jones. I kept reading until I had finished the first part. Having been enriched, I thought I'd also read on in the supplemental chapters. I arrived at page 160 eager to go to the next page…and then things got a bit fuzzy. I could not seem to put what I was reading in sequence and soon discovered that pages were missing. My book went from page 160 directly to page 165. After page 168 it returned to page 161.

I called Sheila, concerned that the printer had messed up the entire order. After checking around, it seems my book was an anomaly…numbered differently from all the others. I laughed, as it seemed sort of fitting with circumstances in which I often find myself.

If there is a mismatched shoe at the store, it seems it will be in my box. If there is one rotten potato served each year in a restaurant, I'm quite sure it is mine. I even have gone through a drive-through hamburger place only to receive an empty bun. Often my pages seemed to be numbered differently from others. And such is the way of life for me.

Do the pages of your life seem to be numbered out of sequence or seemingly different from everyone else's? I have often wondered why certain individuals find their pages numbered so differently from what seems to us "the norm." I look around me and see men and women in poverty, others handling illnesses and various forms of suffering. Their pages are often filled with extreme hardship and challenges.

Yesterday I read about a man who had been exonerated after being falsely convicted of a crime thirty-five years ago. He went to prison at age nineteen. He is now fifty-four, nearly my age as a grandmother. It seems so unfair that he "missed out" on his life. Yet, it seems he did not focus on what was "unfair." He had a big smile when he walked out as a free man. His response was that he harbored no anger because of his belief in God. The pages of his life were numbered seemingly unfairly, but this was the book he was given. He did not walk out a bitter man, but one eager to take his next steps.

Today I went to a first grade classroom to assist my granddaughter with constructing a gingerbread house. As I looked around at the children, I wondered how the pages of their books are numbered. My youngest son was an orphan until we adopted him at age twelve, and he never would have imagined a parent or grandparent coming to his school, much less participating in such a fun activity. Yet for him, as for all of us, there are more pages to come, and our response to however they are numbered makes all the difference.

This world is filled with troubles and sometimes seems unfair. Yet life on earth is temporary. Where we fix our eyes is of utmost importance. As I attempt in the upcoming chapters to share what I've learned from some of the "misnumbered pages" in my life, they may seem trite in comparison to your situation. Or, you may take pity on me with these "unfortunate circumstances" and laugh out loud. Hopefully they will help you to make sense of some of your own misnumbered pages, as well as bring an occasional smile to your face.

More than this, however, my hope is to point you to Jesus, the master teacher. I will also share the stories of three women and life lessons learned from children and my backyard.

No matter how our pages are numbered, following Jesus will lead us on a path with peace in our heart of hearts, all the way into heaven. He calls us (no matter what happens to us or to anyone else around us) with two simple words, "Follow me."

When There's a Knife in Your Back

"Don't scream; I have a knife."

These chilling words, along with the heavy body draped over my back and sharp stabbing point between my shoulder blades, woke me from a deep sleep at 3 AM one summer morning in 1973. Though it was dark in my bedroom, I had full view of the illuminated clock on my headboard. I soon surmised this was going to be a night I would never forget or worse, never have the opportunity to remember.

Just before I had fallen asleep I had been reading my Bible, but had decided to look at a version I was not familiar with. Down on the floor beside my bed was this Bible, with the bold bronzed words on the cover *New English Bible*. This was different from my familiar and oft used Bible with the plain burgundy leather cover.

This stranger, who lay on top of my back, proceeded to talk. "I know you are a religious person," he said.

I replied, "Yes, God is my life. He is my everything and for what you are doing, you will account to God."

Going through my mind were numerous thoughts. I quickly realized I was all alone except for this stranger. My parents' room was far away at the end of a very long ranch style home. Also my mother wore an earpiece for a cochlear implant during the day and would have taken it off for the night, leaving her completely deaf. Besides, if I screamed, I feared I would be killed.

I prayed.

Bible stories I'd read over and over flooded my mind. I remembered David and Goliath, Joshua and Jericho, and Daniel and the lions' den. The faith level in my heart of hearts was tested; absolutely tested to the core as I pondered…"Do I really, really believe God is real; God is alive; God is with me; God can hear me; God can do anything?"

I prayed, "God, can you hear me? Please get me out of this mess!" I was in an impossible situation.

I believed God could save me but also surmised that just as Shadrach, Meshach and Abednego went into the furnace believing God was able, they also went in not knowing if they would come out alive. Whatever the outcome, I knew he was able to save me from this terrifying predicament if he so chose. I also realized it was possible I was breathing my last few breaths.

An hour's worth of conversation ensued. I know because my only view was of the clock. I never saw this person's face, for which I am grateful. I only knew he smoked (because I could smell it) and that he rode a motorcycle (because I heard it leave).

He asked me my name. I then had scriptures going through my head such as "do not lie." I didn't want him to know my name, but having just asked God to spare my life, I was not going to disobey him and lie.

The first answer that came to my mind was from a nursery rhyme: "What's your name? Puddin' Tain. Ask me again and I'll tell you the same." That is the honest truth. I did have the presence of mind to realize quoting that might enrage him, so I answered with a part of my name (my given first name) that I never use.

He asked if I was afraid, to which I answered, "No." By some miracle from God I was not afraid at the time. He told me not to look at him, as he would be ashamed. I was happy to honor that request.

He then told me in graphic detail what he planned to do to me. I told him that was very wrong and he would answer to God for it. He then verbally lessened the intensity of his plan of what he would do to me. I told him that was still wrong and he needed to leave. I talked some about my faith and of God's omnipotence and told him he needed to get his life right with God.

The man explained that he was the "peeping Tom" who

had come months before when my parents were out of town. I had seen someone in the bushes and called the police.

On the night he broke in, we had a guest staying with us (also sleeping on the other side of the house). Since she was to return from Disney World late that night, we had left the door open for her. Then she failed to lock it when she came in.

Near the end of a very long hour the man told me, "I came in here to do everything to you that you have ever heard about or read about. I'm going to leave, and I don't know why. Count to ten and lock the door." He got up and walked out of the room.

For some seemingly insane reason I called out to him and said, "Wait...don't you ever, ever do this to anyone again!"

I heard the door close, counted only to three, got up and locked it and ran to my parents' room to wake them. I must have been a mess, shaking and barely intelligible. My dad quickly called the police who came and took testimony and many fingerprints. However, the most comforting thing to me was that as we waited, my dad just prayed with me. I had not been harmed at all, and there was so much to be grateful for. I begged God for safety and calming of the fear that had now arisen. (After the man had left and the ordeal was over, I found that peace was more difficult to find.)

I learn from this situation that it is often in the darkest, bleakest hours that our faith is tested the most and is needed the most. Do we really, really believe that God is alive, that he is within earshot? Do we really, really believe he will listen to us? Do we believe he is able to do anything? Do we trust that no matter how things come out, God is still the Almighty God? This is what I wrestled with in my heart; and faith was victorious.

> Consequently, faith comes from hearing the message, and the message is heard through the word of Christ. (Romans 10:17)

The Scriptures that had been written on my heart since my youth produced the faith that walked me through this valley of the shadow of death and allowed me to fear no evil, for God was with me. His rod and staff, they comforted me.

When Your Horse Lies Down in the River

It was a carefree, fun-filled time when as a teenage kid I was riding the trails with a few friends in the more than warm Florida afternoon. The horse I was perched atop was quite clever, as well as keenly aware of the heat. We approached a place in the trail where to move forward, all horses had to wade through a small river. I was near the end of the horse parade. When my horse was midstream, she suddenly decided she needed some cool refreshment and lay down in the water.

When your horse lies down in a river and your feet are in the stirrups, you get quite wet. I remember laughing a lot...and then several thoughts came rushing to mind. They included..."You are a stupid horse" and "Why does everyone else's horse do as they are supposed to and I get the stubborn one?" and "You have ruined my ride; I'm all wet and I'll have to quit."

Though only an intermediate rider at best, I have had times when a horse has been so slow I could not get it to move despite my prodding. I have ridden horses where my inexperience made long trots very painful. I have been thrown from a horse, kicked by a horse, ridden into brush. I have had gallops that were exhilarating and those during which I hung on for dear life. All these times I did my best to control the horse. Often I could guide it, but at times unforeseen circumstances made the ride different from what I intended. Isn't this often what happens in our "life ride"?

This simple reflection upon the horse that lay down can remind us of the choices we have in responding to places life takes us, big or small. Often, we are more prepared for the big situations than we are for the smaller everyday occurrences that life throws at us.

So, what's in this cup of learning?

> This day I call heaven and earth as witnesses against you that I have set before you life and death, blessings and curses. Now choose life, so that you and your children may live. (Deuteronomy 30:19)

In most situations in our lives two voices compete for our ear. One is the voice of God; the other is the voice of Satan. This is such a simple concept, often made more complicated than needed. How different life would be if

Eve had chosen to obey the voice of God instead of the seductive lies of the devil. What if Cain, when Satan was crouching at his door, had seen his need to learn from his brother's example, instead of allowing greed and jealousy to provoke him to kill his brother?

Job, in his trials instead of saying "The Lord gives, the Lord takes away. Blessed be the name of the Lord," could have chosen to say, "God hates me and is mean. I'll curse him and die."

What if Jesus had not had the Scriptures on his heart to quickly reply with "It is written…" when hearing the persuasive voice of the devil? How tempting it would have been to say, "You wanna see what I can do, you little dweeb?!!"

Upon being jailed, Paul might have written a very different letter to the Philippians had he not been centered on making the right and spiritual choice. Instead of the amazing selfless attitude, gratefulness and seeing the hand of God opening new, but unexpected doors of opportunity, it might have read,

> Every time I think of what happened to me I get more and more ticked. I'm trying to do good and what do I get? Prison! Life can't get more unfair than that. People are jealous and stirring up trouble while I'm sitting here in prison. There's sure no opportunity

to share about Jesus in this situation. On top of that, Euodia and Syntyche are arguing with each other. Can't you just get along?

Nobody even cares about me except Timothy… and now I've got to send him back to you, you whiny people. And you might as well get Epaphras as well since no one else cares. I just wish I were dead. It would be better.

Or consider Mary's song in Luke:

And Mary said:
"My soul glorifies the Lord
    and my spirit rejoices in God my Savior,
for he has been mindful
    of the humble state of his servant
From now on all generations will call me blessed,
    for the Mighty One has done great things for
        me—
holy is his name." (Luke 1:46–49)

She could have said instead…

"Everything in me questions God.
    My life is ruined and over.
Who does he think he is? What has he done to me?
    From here on out everyone will think terrible
        things about me.
He has ruined me!"

I know I would be tempted to respond this way, letting frustration, anger and faithlessness rule. I learn that the choices I make in my thinking and actions in the smaller things today are key to how I will respond to bigger things of the future.

Each situation we face allows us an opportunity to listen, to learn and to choose life. May you be victorious, albeit wet, when "your horse" lies down in the stream. May you choose well as you look at life and ask, "Where is God in this? Where is Satan? Who will I choose and what will I learn?"

When Your Beatles Cards Fly

According to my sister, I kept looking at my scraped arm, saying over and over again, "I think I hurt my arm." Little did I know my arm should have been the least of my concerns. I don't remember any of this conversation that I had as I was on the road to the hospital. My first remembrance was my family surrounding a hospital bed that for some reason I was in.

I soon learned I had been found earlier that day, lying unconscious in a ravine by the side of the road at the bottom of a steep hill. Certainly, my arm was not the issue of concern.

I would spend the next week in the hospital, going through numerous neurological tests to determine the extent of my head injuries. I remember being wired for an EEG to test my brain and thinking perhaps I should recite the multiplication tables I had learned so that I could "pass the test."

My parents did not let me look into a mirror for a while. The sight was definitively not attractive as my eyes were swollen shut. Rearranged eyebrows and black and blue coloring were various reminders of the recent trauma to my head.

I had been on my way to my cousin's house to trade Beatles cards. When I was a young girl, the Beatles (of the John Lennon, Paul McCartney, George Harrison, Ringo Starr variety) were new and exciting, and I was an avid fan. You could buy little packs of Beatles cards similar to baseball cards. I collected their memorabilia and was on my way to do some trading with cards in my bicycle's back baskets.

On the way to my cousin's house was a large, steep hill. As I sped down it, I realized that my cards were flying out of the basket into the wind. I looked back and that's the last I remember. I was told that an hour later a neighborhood friend discovered my unconscious body. She called my family, and I was soon on the way to the hospital.

Looking back can have drastic consequences. I certainly didn't realize as I was speeding downhill that a pile of leaves was about to be in my path. It seems I thought what was happening behind me was more significant than what was ahead of me.

I should have taken a lesson from Lot's wife. In the account of Lot and his family, God (via angels) told Lot to take his family from Sodom because God planned to destroy the unrepentant city. He promised to take care of Lot and his family because of Lot's faith and righteous life.

> As soon as they had brought them out, one of them said, "Flee for your lives! Don't look back, and don't stop anywhere in the plain! Flee to the mountains or you will be swept away!" (Genesis 19:17)

What would it take for you and me to obey that kind of a command? It would likely be hard to do without just a little peek. After all, life as we knew it was back there. Also there would be a spectacle of fireworks we would not want to miss.

God allowed Lot to run to Zoar because his faith was too little to go farther. Once they safely reached Zoar, God rained down sulfur and destroyed the cities and everything in them. At that point Lot's wife looked back and became a pillar of salt (Genesis 19:26). Wow! She was hardened (in the literal and figurative sense) by the world behind her.

The consequences of my looking back resulted from carelessness about what was ahead of me, as well as being overly concerned with the value of what I was "losing."

Lot's wife was not only careless in not being focused on the safety that God had revealed was ahead, but she also didn't take seriously God's commands. She had too much attachment to the things of this world, and looked back at them when she needed to be steadily and swiftly moving forward.

Learning through reflection is often needed and helpful, but looking back with longing or regret can trap us and keep us from going forward with God. It can paralyze us, embitter us in the attitude of our hearts, and can divide our devotion.

We can become enamored with the world we left for God, or else fearful of repeating mistakes we made in the past. We can encamp on injustices and grow bitter. We can also be fearful of moving forward to what is not known or is not comfortable to us. In all these ways, looking back can have serious consequences.

When we start looking back we fail to see and accept God's guidance. He calls us to look ahead toward what is most valuable. Paul could have had many reasons for looking back and losing his perspective, but through faith, he pressed on.

> But whatever was to my profit I now consider loss for the sake of Christ. What is more, I consider everything a loss compared to the surpassing greatness of knowing Christ Jesus my Lord, for whose sake I have lost all things. I consider them rubbish, that I may gain Christ and be found in him, not having a righteousness

> of my own that comes from the law, but that which is through faith in Christ—the righteousness that comes from God and is by faith.
>
> Not that I have already obtained all this, or have already been made perfect, but I press on to take hold of that for which Christ Jesus took hold of me. Brothers, I do not consider myself yet to have taken hold of it. But one thing I do: Forgetting what is behind and straining toward what is ahead, I press on toward the goal to win the prize for which God has called me heavenward in Christ Jesus.
>
> All of us who are mature should take such a view of things. And if on some point you think differently, that too God will make clear to you. (Philippians 3:7–9, 12–15)

Looking forward means learning lessons from the past but embarking on a journey of faith with a new perspective and a new beginning. It means making peace with my past so that I can access the future and be emotionally available to forge ahead. The ability to start anew is a gift from God.

God calls us to look forward. If I had looked forward as I was cruising down the hill, I would never have experienced such a devastating fall. The Beatles cards were simply not worth it. Is whatever you look back to really worth it?

When Your Sand Dollar Crumbles

The waves were crashing at my feet, and the sand felt wonderfully warm beneath my toes. I was laughing and running on the beach along with several high school friends. We were dreaming of the future as we were preparing to enter college in the fall. Celebrating our graduation and sharing dreams of the upcoming new era, we had walked, talked and ridden the swirling waves for quite some time.

While on our walk, I had the good fortune of finding a beautiful sand dollar, delicate and perfectly shaped. I was eager to put it with my belongings back at the cottage, where we were headed to clean up and prepare for dinner.

Suddenly the clouds thickened. It became obvious a storm was brewing over the ocean. Afternoon thunderstorms were regular occurrences this time of year, but they usually passed quickly.

The sky grew darker, and we started to hear the not-so-faint rumblings of thunder. We wisely decided to quicken our pace in order to reach shelter from the pending storm. We could already see flickers of lightning in the distance.

In a seeming instant, the thunder roared more loudly, and streaks of lightning flashed fiercely across the horizon. We began to run as fast as we could.

I don't know how much time lapsed, but the next thing I remember was being horizontal, sprawled across the sand, skin burning and feeling quite "electric." I opened my eyes, looked around and wondered if I was dead or alive. I then reasoned that the fact that I was asking myself a question probably indicated the latter. I remember feeling sad as I looked down to discover that my beautiful sand dollar was crumbled into tiny jagged pieces inside my clasped hand.

My friends, also face down across the sand, began to raise their heads and look around. We were not sure what had happened. We were all bruised and somewhat bloodied from the impact of our instantaneous fall on the sand. Lightning had struck the shore beside us and knocked us all out cold.

I remember being so happy to be alive and yet realizing only a few inches had stood between me and death. I also reasoned that this would be a very painless, unsuspecting way to go—we never felt a thing.

Standing up, we realized how quickly we had gone

down. We all had "battle wounds"—our legs and knees were particularly affected, as if we had fallen off a skateboard.

> Why, you do not even know what will happen tomorrow. What is your life? You are a mist that appears for a little while and then vanishes. (James 4:14)

I am not promised tomorrow. Compared to eternity, even a long life on earth is as a mist. The older I get the more real this truth becomes. I have lost family and friends who have lived a long life, and others for whom it seemed life had barely begun. A young woman at the time of this shocking experience, I realized that I was not indestructible. Time on earth is short, and we often spend our time, money and imagination as though it will never end. Eternity is what really matters; it lasts beyond time.

I need to make sure I am ready to meet the Lord at all times, and as the Scriptures teach, I need to "store up treasures in heaven, not on earth where moth and rust destroy." The treasures we clutch in our hand today will one day break into pieces. In the face of an eternal perspective, things that seem so important lose their significance. It really did not matter that my sand dollar broke. Yet how much time and worry do I waste focusing on such things in life?

What did you wake up thinking about today? What are your worries? What did you spend your time and money on? Will this matter a hundred years from now?

My once prized and then broken sand dollar meant nothing to me that afternoon. Nothing mattered more in that moment than my relationship with God. Next to that was my relationship with my loved ones and friends. I desire to live each day right with God and with people. One day will be my last day. Then, nothing else will matter.

When Your Doggie Bag Breaks

"Family night" at the Shaw house was always a special time. One night when our kids were in elementary and middle school, we were enjoying a ride to New Hampshire to eat at the Ponderosa Steakhouse. Piled into the minivan, we sang and talked along the way on this cold January evening. Earlier, I had picked up brochures for an upcoming women's event at church and had carefully placed them on the floor of the passenger side where I was sitting.

Sam, our youngest at the time, was particularly quiet on the ride to the restaurant. I inquired as to the reason for his unusually calm demeanor and learned that he was not feeling very well. I assumed he was carsick, as that was a common occurrence in our household.

We arrived and ordered our meals. Trying to enjoy the evening, he ate just a little and lay on the cushion of the booth where we sat. Figuring we should get him back home, we cut the evening short and began the trek back.

Before leaving the restaurant, I decided to be ultra prepared for what might come as I requested several "doggie bags" from the restaurant. These were similar to the little white bags in the pouches on the back of airplane seats. I was feeling quite happy with myself for remembering to request these in case Sam were to get sick on the way home.

I traded seats with Sam, surmising it would be much more comfortable for him to sit up front. As I had suspected, a few miles down the road it became clear that at least one of the little bags would be put to good use. Like a good mom, I leaned over to hold the bag as he filled it with a variety of not-so-pleasant recently-eaten food items.

Carefully, I folded the bag over and pushed down the little clasps, feeling pretty proud of my advance preparation. I would store the bag away until we could pull off at an exit and find a trash can.

Ever so quickly, I transferred the bag from the front seat to the back, with one small problem. As the bag was en route from front seat to back and directly over Sam's head, the bottom burst open. Vomit poured down his head, into the seat belt gears, gracefully cascading down to the brochures fresh from the press.

Immediately a chain reaction went into effect, and the girls began gagging. Wyndham didn't know what had just happened, but pulled over as everyone piled out. Poor little Sam didn't know what had just hit, but he knew life was not good anymore.

In the freezing cold, he began peeling off articles of clothing. It was such a disgusting, nasty scene with children gagging and teary; I didn't know quite what else to do but to laugh hysterically. I know it probably wasn't very sensitive. It just happened.

What can I learn from this experience? I trusted in my own ingenuity and planning, and took great pride in them. I was so confident, but I was so not in control of the situation!

I think of an Old Testament scripture and a New Testament scripture, with similar messages.

> Pride goes before destruction,
>   a haughty spirit before a fall.
>   (Proverbs 16:18)

> So, if you think you are standing firm, be careful that you don't fall! No temptation has seized you except what is common to man. And God is faithful; he will not let you be tempted beyond what you can bear. But when you are tempted, he will also provide a way out so that you can stand up under it. (1 Corinthians 10:12–13)

It is often when things are going well that I can lessen

my dependence on God. I can go through the disciplines of spiritual life, which are important, but then become negligent in digging into the Scriptures and holding to God in prayer. Life is not predictable, and we need to be relying on God day by day. In this world we will have trouble.

> "I have told you these things, so that in me you may have peace. In this world you will have trouble. But take heart! I have overcome the world." (John 16:33)

Satan is always looking for an "opportune time" to send temptations our way.

> When the devil had finished all this tempting, he left him until an opportune time. (Luke 4:13)

It's easy to think I'm all set, extra prepared, and then forget that God is the one who I need to let be in control of my life.

I'm never exempt from or beyond messing up. I must stay dependent in my relationship with God. If I rely on myself and feel in control of my situation, I can easily become prideful. I was proud of myself for being so prepared in the car with Sam, but I ended up with spilled vomit and a real mess.

When Your Hairdresser Speaks a Different Language

8

West Texas in summertime gives a new meaning to the word "hot." This particular summer my husband was finishing his master's degree in Abilene, Texas. One day the temperature was so high I fried an egg on the sidewalk outside of the room we rented. I had heard that was possible, and I learned that indeed it is.

Seven months pregnant, swollen and tired, I was trying my best to stay cool. We were new to the area and unaware of local places to shop and do business. I called a friend to play some tennis. Considering the heat, I pulled my hair back to get some relief from the sweltering conditions.

Later that afternoon, after the tennis, I ventured out with my friend to get my split ends cut. I have noticed that when pregnancy neared its final stages, I often felt a need to have everything in order, down to the ends of my hair. We drove around a bit and found a local hair salon.

After entering, I soon realized that Spanish was the language spoken at this particular salon. Unfortunately, I had taken French in high school.

I figured it could not be too difficult to communicate that I needed my hair trimmed an inch. So, with charade-like motions, I told the hair "butcher"—did I say that? I meant stylist—that I needed my hair trimmed one inch. I used my thumb and forefinger to visualize the amount of hair I meant.

The woman smiled and sat me in her chair. I put my feet out, eager to enjoy the hair wash and pampering that would follow. My friend sat in a chair across from me. With scissors in hand the woman began.

In a few minutes my friend gasped, wide eyed, and let out some form of scream that told me something was not right. I was not facing the mirror, so I was oblivious to the goings on around me. I swung around and to my utter dismay this woman had trimmed my hair one inch all right... unfortunately in the communication mishap she thought I wanted my hair one inch long! I was flabbergasted (meaning really not happy at all)!

The deed was done. It was too late to turn back. The only thing more unfortunate than being seven months pregnant and swollen was being seven months pregnant, swollen and nearly bald! I did the only reasonable thing to do. I began to sob.

My friend tried to comfort me, to no avail. I was so upset I did not want to pay for the haircut, but I had to anyway. I think I would have preferred to torch the shop. I stopped at the store on the way home, got a paper grocery bag, made two holes for my eyes and put it over my head. I really did.

I walked in and my perceptive husband knew through my tears (and the paper bag on my head) that I wasn't happy with the outcome. I'm sure he was shocked. Had I not had poor vision because of the bag on my head, I imagine I would have seen the dismay in his eyes. He always liked longer hair. However, he was kind. He hugged me and assured me it would grow back and that I was beautiful to him.

My disastrous haircut reminds me of a situation described in Joshua 22:10–29. Actions and words that are misunderstood can cause dire consequences.

Three of the Israelite tribes had built an imposing altar on one side of the Jordan River. The other tribes heard about the altar and assumed, because of some other situations that had happened, that it was built in rebellion to God and in decision to go to war against them.

Fortunately, they sent representatives to talk and learned that the altar was actually built to be a witness between the three tribes and the other Israelites to encourage the later generations to always follow the Lord.

Kinsmen almost went to war because of what they thought the other meant.

I have learned that when I speak, I can have a clear understanding in my own mind, but the other party may have an entirely different understanding of what I said. Their response then reflects what they thought I meant. I can react to their response, and we are off to an unpleasant misunderstanding. I realize how careful I need to be to ensure that my communication is clear and that my listener and I are on the same page.

People react, as I do, in ways that make sense to them. Our life stories often give the words we speak different meanings to someone with a different life story. How many times have even married couples, who know each other very well, misinterpreted the words of their spouse by the things going on in their own head when they heard those words?

Along with being careful with my own communication, I also need to remember that when I am bothered by another's words, Jesus tells me to go back to the person directly and seek to settle matters quickly (Matthew 5:23–26, 18:15–17).

Sometimes we just need clarification; other times we need mediation where someone listens to what both parties are feeling and saying (Proverbs 18:17). Outside parties, who can hear without vested emotion, are often helpful, as the Scriptures teach.

Remember, if you aren't careful with your communication, you may end up leaving others with impressions you did not intend. I had thought the communication about my haircut was very clear, yet a shocking glance in the mirror at the beauty salon proved otherwise.

Take the time and trouble to understand what others are trying to say to you as well as to communicate with others. Otherwise, like me, you may not like the end result.

When the Toddler Falls Out

The day had been so encouraging. I had just finished leading a Bible discussion group that morning. It had been lively and productive, and I had a new friend come with me who was eager to continue the discussion as I drove her home. We went from the classroom to my car and buckled her three-year-old into the car seat in the back. He had enjoyed an active, fun-filled learning time with the other children who were there. My children were a bit older and in school at the time, so they weren't with me.

We got into the car, and I locked the doors as we prepared for the ride home. We picked up on our previous discussion of the morning as I got to know my new friend.

On the route home, we had to pass through an area known as "five points." This was an extremely busy intersection that had five converging roads—thus the name.

Just as I was pulling through the intersection, I heard a strange noise. It sounded like a door opening, and then a thump. I glanced toward the back seat. Dismayed and shocked, I barely caught sight of what had just happened.

"Houdini," who was belted in the car seat (in the 1970s they were not built like they are today) in the back of the locked car, had quietly finagled his way out of the seat, unlocked the door and opened it. He had fallen out of the car! All I could see was this precious little boy rolling from my car onto the asphalt with cars coming and going on all sides.

With no time to think I slammed on the brakes while blasting the horn. Once stopped, we jumped out of the car, ran to him, and I grabbed him and put him back into the car. It seemed as if the world stood still at that moment. As the angels would have it, everyone around had stopped immediately.

Next, the mother looked at me and said, "I have epilepsy and I'm about to have a seizure."

I'm sure it was not the sensitive thing to say, but I looked at her, put my arms on her shoulders and said, "Don't you dare! Not now. This is not the time!" And amazingly, she didn't.

A police officer was a few cars behind me, as was a nurse, who immediately checked him out. Thankfully, he was unscathed; not even a scratch. We put him back in the car with Mom by his side and drove home.

What can I learn from such a harrowing experience? I never know what is "around the corner."

I know God's angels were with my backseat traveler that day. I am grateful there were no cell phones then so that everyone around me was more alert. Distraction could have produced tragedy on this day, but thankfully he was not hurt.

When the unexpected happens, it is so easy for me to want to fall apart and let my emotions rule instead of taking my thoughts captive.

When a loved one is sick, I can imagine the worst situation that could happen. An unknown illness can bring on preplanning my funeral. I can worry about the simplest of things. These thoughts distract me and keep me from relying on God.

Peter reminds me to be alert and self-controlled:

> Therefore, prepare your minds for action; be self-controlled; set your hope fully on the grace to be given you when Jesus Christ is revealed. (1 Peter 1:13)

The King James Version of the Bible has an interesting translation of the above verse, giving me a vivid image:

> Wherefore gird up the loins of your mind, be sober, and hope to the end for the grace that is to be brought unto you at the revelation of Jesus Christ.

This verb "gird" is from the same root as the word for "girdle." Have you ever put on a girdle? It is used to tone and smooth out otherwise "flabby" areas around our midsection and/or back section. A girdle is not easy to put on. You have to "fight your body" to pull it up and into position.

I love the image of putting a girdle around the "loins of my mind." It tells me I need to put controls around my thoughts instead of letting my mind become "flabby." However, it's not easy. The "muffin tops" of our mind keep trying to fight their way out!

The wisdom of God teaches me to be mentally and spiritually alert and then to get busy putting spiritual thinking into action. Spiritually, do we let our mind wander and flap in the breeze, or do we make the effort as the Scriptures teach to take our thoughts captive and make them obedient to Christ? (2 Corinthians 10:5). This is not easy to do and takes putting the Scriptures into our minds, disciplining our time—plus praying and getting help from others who are also trying to live the same way.

Just as alertness in retrieving the boy could have saved his life, being spiritually alert and prepared can save our soul, as well as the souls of others.

> But in your hearts set apart Christ as Lord. Always be prepared to give an answer to everyone who asks you to give the reason for the hope that you have. But do this with gentleness and respect. (1 Peter 3:15)

When You Pack the Trash Bag

I love winters in New England. One of my favorite scenes includes swirling snow, a roaring fire, a book and, of course, the hot cup of coffee. These make for an ideal day.

On wintery days such as this, our public schools sometimes consider skiing part of physical education. With parents' permission, a bus takes the kids to a local ski area one afternoon a week, and they learn to ski. At least that was the case nearly fifteen years ago when my older daughter was in high school.

Having learned to ski on the school outings and eager to enjoy some winter fun, she signed up for an extended ski outing with a group from church. Before catching the bus, Melissa came by the house to pick up her ski clothing, which she had packed earlier in a "sleek" black plastic trash bag.

Unbeknownst to her, I had collected trash that day and had put it in a big black plastic trash bag.

You can imagine Melissa's surprise when, while on the bus, she reached in to grab her gloves and instead pulled out a handful of coffee grounds. She had taken my bag of trash with her on the bus. This was the 90s, and we didn't have cell phones. Prospects were looking bleak for her adventure.

Meanwhile, I was just as surprised when I glanced into the trash bag and discovered Melissa's belongings. I had a moment of panic, felt bad for Melissa, and then my morbid humor came out with hearty laughter as I pictured her pulling out trash at the ski lodge. (Sorry—sort of—Melissa.)

Fortunately, I was able to pull it together, gather the trash bag full of clothes, and drive to the ski area, which was about an hour away. Melissa was relieved to see me walking toward her with the authentic clothes trash bag. I took the useless bag of trash to the dumpster where it belonged, and she was able to enjoy the outing.

But whatever was to my profit I now consider loss for the sake of Christ. What is more, I consider everything a loss compared to the surpassing greatness of knowing Christ Jesus my Lord, for whose sake I have lost all things. I consider them rubbish, that I may gain Christ and be found in him, not having a righteousness of my own that comes from the law, but that which is

> through faith in Christ—the righteousness that comes
> from God and is by faith. (Philippians 3:7–9)

It's so easy to go about our lives carrying a bag of rub-bish with us. While thinking it has everything we need, we don't realize it is simply trash! How often do we hold on to worldly thinking, accomplishments or possessions thinking they are fulfilling and what we need? Then when the time comes to deal with life's challenges, we find them useless.

When we are confronted with the temptation to lie or to be impure, how much will stylish new clothes help us? How about our education from the finest schools? Will it help us overcome the loss, rejection and guilt that we will face? When a loved one passes or we are faced with a seri-ous illness, will the "pedigree" of our family or the amount of money in our bank account be what brings us peace? Will a promotion at work or popularity in our school for-give us of our sins and shortcomings?

In the above passage of Scripture, the apostle Paul re-minds me that nothing in this world can compare with my relationship with Jesus.

Jesus teaches me that whatever the world has to offer is really just garbage. And he didn't drive sixty minutes to exchange bags with me. He went all the way to the cross, and in his death left me the glorious new bag of forgive-ness, relationship and eternal life.

When There's a
Black Glove

We had only been married a few months and life was good. Wyndham and I lived in a little garage apartment. The bathroom was located between the living room and our bedroom, with entrance doors from each of those rooms.

We were busy leading a campus ministry while I was also finishing my last quarter of college with an out-of-state internship that I had previously arranged with the university. Our schedules were a bit crazy. I had to work in the afternoon until 9 PM and then go to campus to lead a women's Bible discussion. Wyndham would be gone most evenings, so we were coming and going often.

One afternoon or evening, I don't remember which, Wyndham had to leave the house soon after I arrived. We told each other goodbye and looked forward to time together later. After leaving, he realized he had forgotten something and came back into the apartment to get it. Meanwhile, I was sudsing away in the shower.

Upon his return, he realized I was in the shower and

thought it would be hilarious to play a practical joke on me. So, he grabbed a black glove, sneaked into the bathroom and dangled his glove-clad hand over the shower door—I'm sure he was barely able to contain his enthusiasm for this wonderful joke.

Do you remember the earlier chapter entitled, "When There's a Knife in Your Back"? Apparently he had not read it…

As you can imagine, I did not find this funny. As I melted in a puddle of tears on the shower floor, my very penitent husband did his best to console me. He felt terrible. I forgave him, and he never did anything like that again.

Fear is powerful. It can dominate and even control us if not checked. Evil in the world creates a lot of terror and sometimes causes fear to harbor in our hearts. Current experiences can trigger anxious emotions from previous frightening or difficult experiences that are in no way related.

When I understand God and rest in his presence, I can be at peace. Without God, I am a very fearful person. My vivid imagination can create dilemmas and dire circumstances that have not happened and probably never will happen. I can receive so much negative information via news and media that the "what ifs" can start creeping into the crevices of my mind. Worry can then take me captive. I take heart and gain hope in these scriptures:

> For you did not receive a spirit that makes you a slave again to fear, but you received the Spirit of sonship. And by him we cry, "Abba, Father." (Romans 8:15)

> There is no fear in love. But perfect love drives out fear, because fear has to do with punishment. The one who fears is not made perfect in love. (1 John 4:18)

These verses have been incredibly instrumental in helping me learn to trust God's love and not to fear what might happen. I have also learned from these scriptures the kind of openness, honesty and kindness I need to practice in my relationships with others. Situations that bring up fear can feel like "the black glove of death." But on closer look, that glove may actually contain the hand of someone who loves me more than any other. And certainly God will work through any glove that appears in our life. He promises us so.

When Your Teacher Goes Nuts

Mrs. P was known as the "grammar queen." Since she was my English teacher in seventh grade, I knew that having her again in the ninth grade was going to mean hard work. She drilled us with English grammar, something I now appreciate. My older sisters had also had her as a teacher. Being an overachiever of sorts, I did well in her class, and given her history with me and my sisters, she treated me as sort of a "favorite," I suppose.

Every day Mrs. P gave homework. As she began her class, she went through the roll call, and her students were to answer with the words "prepared" or "unprepared." Nothing else. Prepared meant you had completed your homework. Unprepared meant you had not.

On this particular day nothing seemed different in the classroom. As she called the roll, I had my word ready as she neared the end of the alphabet.

"Prepared," I answered.

I'll never forget the next series of events. She glared at me and asked, "What did you say?"

I carefully repeated my answer: "Prepared!"

At that moment something came unglued for her. She came to my desk, picked up my books and threw them to the back of the room. Grabbing me by the arm and taking me into the hall, she started banging my head against the lockers and repeating the words, "I know your scheme; you are out to get me! You have a plot against me!"

One of my friends ran out to help me, and Mrs. P screamed at her, "You're expelled!"

A few moments later a counselor came to intervene and took me away to her office to comfort me as I was a crying mess. I don't know what she did with the teacher. My mother came to pick me up and took me home. I felt at that moment I would never darken the doors of the school again.

However, time helped ease the shock of that day, and a few days later I was back at school and in her class. The teacher, who had been confronted, had absolutely no remembrance of her actions. (Scary, I know.) Today she would not have her job, but in the 60s things were a bit different. Lawsuits didn't fly freely. I did hear that several years later a similar instance happened, after which she swiftly retired.

I was a good student; I did my homework; I was respectful to my teacher. It was unfair that she treated me the way she did. But what this reminds me is that life is full of unfair.

If I get overly concerned about fairness, I am in for great disappointment. Mrs. P was mean, scary and not fair. However, retaliation or bitterness mostly hurts the one from whom it comes. What a shame it would have been if I failed to go back to school, began to mistrust all teachers, and created a gossip chain...and meanwhile Mrs. P is totally oblivious to anything she did wrong. Isn't that the way it often is? We can stew and complain while the other party is completely unaware and we are being eaten away by the acid of bitterness.

I treasure the story of Joseph in Genesis. It is my all-time favorite of one who is mistreated and yet continues to trust in God. Thrown into a pit and left to die by his brothers, falsely accused of sexual misconduct by Potiphar's wife, thrown into prison and lied to by inmates, he suffered injustice after injustice.

Most meaningful, however, is learning from the attitude of Jesus, who was misunderstood and mistreated time and time again, even to death. He was shown complete injustice; he was absolutely sinless yet hung on a cross. Even to his last breath he did not become bitter or resentful even one time. Instead, he trusted God who judges justly, and he always thought of our good.

> But how is it to your credit if you receive a beating for doing wrong and endure it? But if you suffer for doing good and you endure it, this is commendable before God. To this you were called, because Christ suffered for you, leaving you an example, that you should follow in his steps.
>
>> "He committed no sin,
>>   and no deceit was found in his mouth."
>
> When they hurled their insults at him, he did not retaliate; when he suffered, he made no threats. Instead, he entrusted himself to him who judges justly. He himself bore our sins in his body on the tree, so that we might die to sins and live for righteousness; by his wounds you have been healed. (1 Peter 2:20–24)

This is a challenging scripture. Whether in the classroom, the hospital, the funeral home or even highway traffic, entrusting ourselves to the one who judges justly is a daily struggle. Jesus did this so that by those wounds I can be healed deep down in my soul.

When You Get Sprayed with Gasoline

This particular Friday was my son Sam's fifth birthday. It was going to be an exciting night at the Boston Garden where our church was meeting to send out numerous mission teams. Our kids were very involved and excited as we had raised and sold puppies to make money to contribute to these teams. We had a puppy named after each city where the teams were going.

Wyndham had already gone to the Garden, and I was driving down with my friend Anita and my three kids. My little blue Hyundai was filled to the max with people, but empty on fuel. I was going to have to get gasoline before we made the trip in to Boston.

Back in the day, gas stations were called service stations because attendants serviced your car while they pumped your gas. I had my window down and asked the attendant to "fill 'er up." This didn't usually take long, as the car only held eleven gallons of gas.

When I was preparing to pay, I noticed I had been charged for twenty-one gallons of gas. I explained to the attendant that there seemed to be a mistake as my tank was not nearly so big. A young guy, he said he couldn't do anything and that I should come back on Monday.

I started my car, and to my surprise my tank still registered empty. I had paid for twenty-one gallons and had none.

I again spoke to the attendant, saying something was wrong with the situation. He looked puzzled as he fiddled with the tall rectangular gas dispenser with one hand and held the nozzle in his other hand.

He then said, "Oh, I see the problem," and ever so quickly pulled the gas lever down, which he had not previously done. Unfortunately, he had also set a lever on the nozzle so it would not have to be pressed in order to dispense gas, but would do so automatically.

As he swung around to push the lever down, the nozzle was pointed directly toward me and my open window. The lever switched, and a full force of gasoline rushed into my face (nostrils, eyes and mouth). My daughter Kristen was doused as well. I screamed in agony from the burning, ran to the bathroom putting my face under the faucet and heard the sirens of the ambulance quickly approaching.

My daughters and Anita had all been sprayed in varying degrees. Kristen's stomach was burned. Anita and my other daughter were fine, and I was in agony!

As the medics were flushing out my eyes, I remember asking one of them about the sign that hung by the station: "Warning: harmful or fatal if swallowed." I told him that I'd swallowed some and asked him if that meant I would die.

He replied, "I don't think so," which at the time didn't seem too comforting. With all the commotion, I did not know what had happened to my son. I asked, and the emergency technician told me the police had him.

As we arrived at the hospital, I was feeling relief that I wasn't dead and was encouraged that Kristen was being treated and was resting comfortably. My eyes were flushed with water for quite a while and fortunately there was no permanent damage.

I'll never forget Sam coming in with the police officer, running over to me and saying, "Mommy, I thought you were going to die and I was going to jail."

Happy birthday, Sam. I felt so sad for him. His five-year-old perspective was terrifying. What a birthday present that was.

Sam thought he was going to jail. That's what the police car meant to him. Also to his little five-year-old understanding, being taken in an ambulance was being taken to death. Fear was inside of him because he didn't have the "big picture" of what was happening.

Things aren't always as they seem. When in our minds things don't make sense (and perhaps in our lifetime never will), God is still at work. The fact that I cannot understand it from my perspective doesn't mean that all is a loss.

I am mindful of two favorite scriptures:

> In the same way, the Spirit helps us in our weakness. We do not know what we ought to pray for, but the Spirit himself intercedes for us with groans that words cannot express. And he who searches our hearts knows the mind of the Spirit, because the Spirit intercedes for the saints in accordance with God's will.
>
> And we know that in all things God works for the good of those who love him, who have been called according to his purpose. (Romans 8:26–28)

> But Joseph said to them, "Don't be afraid. Am I in the place of God? You intended to harm me, but God intended it for good to accomplish what is now being done, the saving of many lives." (Genesis 50:19–20)

I will try to remember and relearn that God is always bigger than I and is at work in ways I don't understand. He can take bad situations and cause his glory to shine.

When Your Friend
Totals Your Car

New friends were sharing a meal at our home. An auto mechanic, the man extended a generous offer. While riding in our car he had noticed that our air conditioner was not working. (Given that it was scorching hot outside, it was not difficult for him to come to this conclusion.) Kindly, he offered to take our car back to his shop to repair it. We were very appreciative of this gracious offer.

A few days later he gave us a call to let us know the air conditioning was completely fixed. Encouraged, we made plans to pick it up the next day. Showing even more kindness, he offered to bring it back to our house that evening.

A few hours later he called us with discouraging news. The good news was that he was completely fine. The bad news was that he had been in an accident and our newly cooled car was totaled. We were thankful he was not hurt, which superseded the disappointment of having a crashed car. We asked him not to worry as it was just a thing, not a person.

Of course he felt terrible about the situation, and he

and his wife invited our family to their place for dinner the next week. I supposed he wanted to make things better and extend his apology again. We were eager to go. It was nice to be invited out. It could have felt intimidating to add our family of five to their dinner table.

We looked forward to the evening, and as we arrived, we were greeted by a small, cute little black-and-white dog. We are dog lovers and always enjoy the furry canine friends. As we were seated in the living room our son Sam (then three years old) dropped something on the floor and proceeded to pick it up. As soon as he leaned over, the seemingly sweet dog became violent and tore into his face. The bleeding was profuse. Sam's lip was completely torn in two; there were gashes on his cheek and blood flowing so strongly from around his eye we could not see what kind of damage had been done.

Grabbing a towel, we put pressure on his face and rushed to the hospital. Soon he was in a straightjacket with twelve shots going into his face and a plastic surgeon beginning his suturing. I can still hear his cries while lying in the jacket; he called out, "Mommy, save me! Get me out of here!" And I had to just stand there and watch.

It took a while for the wounds to heal, but they finally did. Our new friends didn't know what to say. I truly felt bad for them (and felt bad for us as well).

I was inwardly relieved they did not offer to do something else to encourage us. This was becoming too much of a nightmare. Our car was totaled, our son was hurt, and the expense was not small.

I remember two distinct lessons from these misadventures. They are not really related but are meaningful to me.

I have often been drawn closer to the cross of Jesus by remembering how I felt when my son was constrained, getting shot after shot and many stitches. His cry, "Mommy, save me! Get me out of here!" rang in my ears. How much worse was it for God to hear his son say, "My God, my God, why have you forsaken me?" And it was not for his good, but for mine.

For the other lesson, the scripture that somes to mind is a challenging one straight from the mouth of Jesus:

> Then Peter came to Jesus and asked, "Lord, how many times shall I forgive my brother when he sins against me? Up to seven times?"
>
> Jesus answered, "I tell you, not seven times, but seventy-seven times." (Matthew 18:21–22)

I can get fed up when people mess up again and again. It is not easy to put this scripture into practice. Yet, I mess up again and again, and Jesus doesn't tire of offering his mercy. For that I am so grateful. I'm sure there have been many times when God was "driving me" and I've fought for control and swerved, thus "totaling" the spiritual car.

There are times I have "bitten" someone near me (thankfully I've never literally bitten them but certainly have used careless, biting words). God didn't throw me out of the house or decide it was too disappointing to have contact with me again. For this I am eternally grateful.

> The LORD is gracious and compassionate,
>   slow to anger and rich in love. (Psalm 145:8)

When the Doctor Says It's Okay but It's Not

It had been a rough week. Wyndham and I had been busier than usual with our jobs. The school year was coming to a close, and the kids were involved in many activities with church and school. I particularly felt the burden as Wyndham had been sick in bed all week. He was not getting any better. Sam seemingly had caught a terrible stomach virus. He was in major pain.

I realized things were not looking good and drove them both to the doctor's office. This was one of the "McDoctor" type of urgent care facilities. The doctor, upon examining Wyndham, was quite concerned with his grey color, total malaise, fever and horrible cough. Sending him to get x-rays, he quickly surmised that it was pneumonia. I think the doc became distracted while he was deciding whether to send him home or to the hospital. He finally said he could go home as long as he was carefully monitored.

I reminded the doctor that Sam was quite sick and needed to be examined as well. He asked Sam some questions and did a quick exam, stating that he seemed to have a virus. The pain was so severe I inquired as to whether the problem could be his appendix. The doctor said he didn't think so and mentioned he should probably do some blood tests.

However, everyone was feeling so bad he decided instead to send us home so the patients could quickly get back to bed.

Wyndham began his antibiotic regimen, and Sam continued to get worse overnight. His fever increased, and I made a phone call to a friend who was a physician. Upon learning he had just been to the doctor, my friend figured it was just a virus as well.

I still was quite unsettled. I called another of my friends whose child had just recently suffered from appendicitis. She advised me that regardless of what the doctor said, I knew my son best and should do what I believed he needed. I immediately took him to the emergency room. (Thank you, Kay.)

The hospital near our house does not admit children, yet within an hour of our arrival Sam was in surgery for his ruptured appendix. The surgeon told me later how near to death he really was. I was shocked and forlorn, sitting with my sick child while my husband was so ill at home.

For several days I lived in his hospital room, plucking imaginary baseball cards out of the air that morphine had convinced Sam were attacking him.

Several biblical principles help my perspective. Some of my friends asked if we had considered suing the doctor for negligence. I called the doctor to tell him what had happened. He not only came to the hospital to visit, but he also came to our home! While it was tempting to assign blame, that would not have helped the situation. The doctor apologized profusely and was truly mortified by his error.

I must take personal responsibility for my choices. I need to seek advice, but whether that advice is helpful or harmful, it is not constructive to blame the doctor or anyone else who gave the advice. If Sam had not made it, while I'm sure the doctor would have taken some blame, it would not have made a difference in the outcome. I had to take responsibility for what was needed.

Likewise, my spiritual condition, my growth, my making it to heaven, my overcoming struggles is not dependent on anyone else. Other people can hinder or they can help…but I must make the choice to work out my own salvation.

> Therefore, my dear friends, as you have always obeyed—not only in my presence, but now much more in my absence—continue to work out your salvation with fear and trembling, for it is God who works

in you to will and to act according to his good purpose. (Philippians 2:12–13)

A second insight I gained is illustrated in the following
verses:

> "They dress the wound of my people
>   as though it were not serious.
> 'Peace, peace,' they say,
>   when there is no peace.
> Are they ashamed of their loathsome conduct?
>   No, they have no shame at all;
>   they do not even know how to blush.
> So they will fall among the fallen;
>   they will be brought down when I punish them,"
>   says the LORD.

This is what the LORD says:

> "Stand at the crossroads and look;
>   ask for the ancient paths,
> ask where the good way is, and walk in it,
>   and you will find rest for your souls."
>   (Jeremiah 6:14–16)

The doctor dressed Sam's "wound" as though it was
not serious. He didn't want to put him through the pain
and inconvenience of a blood test. However, the prick of a
needle is nothing compared to a ruptured appendix.

Sometimes we don't want to hear the truth or speak the truth because it is painful. As the prophet Jeremiah recounts in this passage, putting Band-Aids on cancer or dressing spiritual wounds lightly for fear of hurting someone can have fatal spiritual consequences.

Finding the truth in our lives does not always, or even often, feel "warm and fuzzy." Addressing the truth (as told by God) in our lives is crucial. Then we "at the crossroads" of our life can decide to walk in the good way and find rest for our souls.

When the Person Beside You Sets Himself on Fire

I lived in West Virginia for three years. The license plates read "Wild, Wonderful West Virginia." It's a place different from any other in which I have lived. Schools in West Virginia take several days off when deer hunting season begins.

I had many wild things happen when we lived there, but one stands out to me.

My husband was the minister for a church during the years that we lived in West Virginia. I loved that in the same congregation were coal miners, professors, people who were illiterate and others who were well-educated, and a number of medical doctors. Diversity is always a product of the family of God. When gathering for communal worship, it is encouraging to see faces of people you don't yet know. This lets you know that more and more people are coming to learn about Jesus.

This particular Sunday a man came and sat down beside me. He had a working dog with him, and I could tell he was blind. The church worshipped together through song and prayer, and then my husband began to preach from the Bible.

I noticed a bit of stirring and fidgeting from the man beside me. I tried not to pay much attention to him, but the distraction became more intense. It seemed he was purposefully pouring water on himself. What my olfactory senses soon communicated to me was that in fact he was pouring gasoline on himself. He proceeded to take a cigarette lighter from his pocket and set himself on fire!

So much for the sermon! I'm not sure what I did, but I think it came out in a scream. Several of us rolled him around on the floor and used whatever sweater or coat we could find to douse the flames.

Evidently, he wasn't trying to commit suicide; he just thought it would be interesting to see what happened. The fire subsided and he was okay. Obviously, he had some mental issues troubling him.

In this situation, and in fact quite a number of other situations, I learn that there are numerous instances where by myself I am helpless to respond. Some issues are beyond my understanding and expertise. I'd like to know all, but I don't.

However, I can always scream for help! This goes against my nature. I'd like to calmly handle everything with a sagacious demeanor that enables me to know just what to do. It takes humility to ask for help, and sometimes that humility doesn't come easy.

> Consider it pure joy, my brothers, whenever you face trials of many kinds, because you know that the testing of your faith develops perseverance. Perseverance must finish its work so that you may be mature and complete, not lacking anything. If any of you lacks wisdom, he should ask God, who gives generously to all without finding fault, and it will be given to him. But when he asks, he must believe and not doubt, because he who doubts is like a wave of the sea, blown and tossed by the wind. That man should not think he will receive anything from the Lord; he is a double-minded man, unstable in all he does. (James 1:2–8)

I love that God assumes we need wisdom and is waiting for us to ask. I so appreciate that when we ask, he doesn't tell us we're stupid or troublesome for needing help. He gives it generously, without finding fault. However, I must have faith that his advice and his wisdom are better than mine and they are what I need.

Do you find it difficult to ask for help? I do for various reasons. I don't like to trouble people. I don't like to inconvenience people. I don't want to be viewed as one who feels entitled. I don't like to make mistakes. I like things neat and tidy and "all figured out."

When I fail to pray and ask God for daily help, it shows most often that I'm relying on myself and doing things out of my own strength. This is both foolish and prideful.

When I fail to ask others for help, it robs them of the joy of serving as well as feeling needed. If people don't feel that I need them, there is no possibility of having a close friendship. Everyone wants to feel needed.

I am reminded by this incendiary incident in West Virginia that "screaming for help" allows for others to feel needed, for teamwork to happen and for more good to be done for more people.

When There's a Deer in Your Bathtub

I mentioned in the previous chapter that in West Virginia I experienced a number of wild things. The state recreation there seems to be hunting. I remember once being in line at a McDonald's drive-through along with several other vehicles who had dead deer strapped atop.

Many, if not most, people loved to hunt deer. They would get up at "o'dark-thirty" in freezing cold weather, climb up into a tree to sit on a little board (known as a tree stand) and wait and wait. Days earlier they would have scoped out the best place for their tree stand by looking for "deer poop." They would even spray themselves with "eau de deer urine" cologne so the deer wouldn't smell them. (Everyone else would, but I guess the deer didn't.) If I sound a bit cynical, it's just that I don't understand this phenomenon.

While my husband assures me that the Disney movie *Bambi* is propaganda and that overpopulation of deer is causing many of them to starve, I still think they are cute and that Bambi talks. I don't want to be near a dead deer, and I won't eat venison. I don't dislike you if it's your thing; it's just not mine. However, I do have some limits which I will explain.

My husband is an outdoorsman to the core. Even tearfully, when our first child was born he exclaimed (referring to the birth process), "Wow, that was just like skinning a rabbit." (Ladies, don't fear…that was over thirty years ago, and he has truly become a sensitive man.)

Rain or shine or extreme temperatures, he is invigorated by being outdoors. Fishing is a thrill, as is hunting, though I am thankful he doesn't particularly enjoy hunting deer. In West Virginia it was a different story. It seemed most of the male population was in the woods on the opening day of deer season.

The hunters hunt by rifle and by bow and arrow. I remember one time Wyndham was practicing his archery in preparation for "bow season." He placed his target (for practice) on a pile of hay in the side yard. Behind our yard was a gravel alley; beyond that were neighbors' homes. Since he was hitting the bull's eye while standing stationary, he decided to make things more challenging by running and shooting.

I guess it was a little too challenging as his arrow missed the target, skipped across the gravel and went through the neighbor's bedroom window. (That was an embarrassing visit to the neighbor's as he had to explain the mishap.) No one was hurt, and the neighbor was kind and even found humor in the situation.

One morning Wyndham had gone out with a bunch of the guys. I was out somewhere with the kids (not hunting, but likely "gathering" at the grocery store). Upon my arrival home I was feeling urgency to get to the bathroom. As soon as I went in, I promptly came out and considered driving somewhere far, far away.

Lying in my bathtub was a skinned deer. That's right; a fully formed deer with no skin…in the bathtub where I bathed our children!! He was skinned, and I was fit to be tied. I know my husband learned from this. But so did I.

People are different. They have different likes, desires and ways of thinking. I am sometimes too quick to pass judgment when someone's thinking is different from mine.

When differences are not matters of doctrine or right or wrong, they are simply preferences. Others' preferences are no better or worse than mine, though by nature I certainly tend to think mine are the "best ones." My husband's love of fishing and hunting is something I don't relate to. For a number of years it was a source of conflict between us. However, if I had not finally come to appreciate our differences and accept them, our marriage would have suffered. Paul's statement to the Christians in Rome helps me in this area:

> Accept one another, then, just as Christ accepted you, in order to bring praise to God. (Romans 15:7)

I am learning more and more to get to know and appreciate those who have interests and preferences that are different from mine. Consider the following scripture:

> Do nothing out of selfish ambition or vain conceit, but in humility consider others better than yourselves. Each of you should look not only to your own interests, but also to the interests of others.
> Your attitude should be the same as that of Christ Jesus. (Philippians 2:3–5)

Do I begrudgingly acknowledge another's interests, or do I put their interests above my own? This is a daily decision and one that is not easy to make. In fact it's hard to do. When I realize my attitude should be the same as that of Christ Jesus, I am humbled and dependent on his words and his spirit to see me through each day.

When You Forget Your Stones of Remembrance

At various significant times in my life I have collected "stones of remembrance." Stones of remembrance are mentioned several times in the Bible, perhaps most notably in Joshua 4:4–7:

> So Joshua called together the twelve men he had appointed from the Israelites, one from each tribe, and said to them, "Go over before the ark of the LORD your God into the middle of the Jordan. Each of you is to take up a stone on his shoulder, according to the number of the tribes of the Israelites, to serve as a sign among you. In the future, when your children ask you, 'What do these stones mean?' tell them that the flow of the Jordan was cut off before the ark of the covenant of the LORD. When it crossed the Jordan, the waters of the Jordan were cut off. These stones are to be a memorial to the people of Israel forever."

Because of this scripture, I have often picked up small rocks or pebbles at particular points in my life. Some of these represent a particularly special time with God, a significant breakthrough or specific blessing. A few have been for meaningful events. However, there are two problems with most of these stones of remembrance: I can't remember where I put them and also I can't remember details on when and why they were collected. Somehow, I'm not thinking this is quite what God had in mind when speaking of stones of remembrance.

However, there are a few stones of remembrance I am sure I will never forget. I've collected five of them so far. They are called kidney stones. The first time I passed a kidney stone I thought I was going to die, and that if I didn't I'd ask for someone to shoot me. On a pain scale of 1 to 10, I'd say the pain was somewhere around a "20."

I've birthed three children, had broken bones (broke my arm climbing stairs with skates on and broke my nose walking into a wall) and various other accidents mentioned throughout this book. These pale in comparison to the kidney stones. Sometimes I've responded to the pain with vomiting and other times with some sort of phenomenon that causes my hands and fingers to writhe and freeze in awkward, spastic configurations. I understand this is caused by pain so intense you forget to breathe. Some people even pass out.

Usually with these stones I've gotten quick attention in the ER in the form of an IV of pain medication. With most of the stones, only a medicine ten times stronger than morphine took the pain away. One stone had to be removed surgically. The last instance, just a few months ago, continued several days. I was able to collect the stone when it passed; I put it in a jar and proudly brought it to the urologist. I "affectionately" referred to it as my stone of remembrance.

I've learned numerous lessons from these stones. The first is that I believe I will always remember them. I won't forget them like I did the other stones because they stopped me in my tracks. Anything and everything I'd planned for the day they emerged was changed; all was superseded by these vicious though small stones. They got my full attention and took my entire focus. I suffered mightily for these stones.

Many things of significance come through pain. Lessons we learn, character that we build, compassion we show, are often results of suffering. Unless we are stopped in our tracks, life can quickly "go on as usual." Paul reminds me that suffering, though difficult, can bring rewards that are eternal in scope:

> Not only so, but we also rejoice in our sufferings, because we know that suffering produces perseverance; perseverance, character; and character,

hope. And hope does not disappoint us, because
God has poured out his love into our hearts by the
Holy Spirit, whom he has given us. (Romans 5:3–5)

Secondly, I am so grateful for the stone's passing and deeply appreciate the relief. There is a reason God asked the Israelites to collect stones and explain to their children the meaning of those stones. They were to be reminders of God's faithfulness to them, which they were then to pass on to others. We can so quickly forget the good, the amazing things God has done, and remember more quickly the difficult times of our struggles.

Sometimes I can get so worried about the future or anxious about how something will work out that I wane in my faith. I can forget the mighty and powerful ways God works in my life. In my lifetime I have seen so many mighty workings of God. As I saw mission teams go to Russia, I saw the iron curtain "ripped apart." About the time our mission team went to Johannesburg, I saw apartheid end. As several disciples went into Germany, the Berlin wall came down. I do have a piece of that wall (a stone of remembrance) in my cabinet. Suddenly, my world history books became obsolete as history took a sharp turn.

I want to take the contents of my cup of learning and pass it on to others around me and those coming after me. The stones of remembrance from our lives are not gathered just so we collect and display them. They serve no purpose unless we pass on their meaning.

Use your stones of remembrance to show God to those around you and to attend to others' needs.

> Praise be to the God and Father of our Lord Jesus Christ, the Father of compassion and the God of all comfort, who comforts us in all our troubles, so that we can comfort those in any trouble with the comfort we ourselves have received from God. For just as the sufferings of Christ flow over into our lives, so also through Christ our comfort overflows. (2 Corinthians 1:3–5)

In our cups are challenges and trials, but also blessings and victories. Let us strive to let the stones bring glory to God and benefit those we touch.

When Your House Is on Fire

Excitement was buzzing throughout the house as my parents and sisters recounted the previous evening's events. I was about ten years old at the time, and it had been a particularly cold night for Florida. My dad had been busy putting outdoor heaters near the citrus trees and covering his well-tended plants with plastic. We were able to enjoy a rare fire in the fireplace that evening before going to bed. Seldom was the weather cool enough to justify building a fire.

After our family was asleep, my parents (and sisters) were awakened by a phone call. Our neighbor had been out after midnight checking on his plants and saw flames on our roof. Alarmed, he immediately notified my parents, who called the fire department. (This was well before the invention of household smoke alarms.) A spark from the fireplace had ignited some of the pine straw on top of the roof, setting the roof on fire.

My dad and neighbor grabbed the garden hose and went on the roof. To their dismay, the water was frozen so they attempted to stomp out and smother the fire that had begun. By the time the fire department arrived most of it had been extinguished.

The next morning as the family gathered for breakfast and recounted the events, I was quite confused. I knew nothing of the excitement of the phone call, the neighbors outside my window, or the stomping above me on the roof. I had no knowledge of a fire engine parked near my room. I had been sound asleep, oblivious to the commotion.

At first I was a bit dismayed that they had let me sleep through all of this. I was assured that they were keenly aware of the timing and progress and would not have hesitated to awaken me and carry me out if the fire had not been contained. I took some comfort in this, but as a young girl I was disappointed to have missed the excitement.

I thought about this series of events as I poured it into my cup of learning. How often I am completely unaware of the workings of God who is busy putting out various types of fires all around me. He is working his great plans before me, but often while I sleep. Even in the darker hours, he is there to comfort me and guide me as the oft quoted twenty-third psalm so eloquently states:

> The LORD is my shepherd, I shall not be in want.
>   He makes me lie down in green pastures,
> he leads me beside quiet waters,
>   he restores my soul.
> He guides me in paths of righteousness
>   for his name's sake.
> Even though I walk
>   through the valley of the shadow of death,
> I will fear no evil,
>   for you are with me;
> your rod and your staff,
>   they comfort me. (Psalm 23:1–4)

It is comforting to learn from so many scriptures that God is at work, always! I may be oblivious to what is going on, but God is not. Here are three more of my favorite passages that teach me this truth:

> He will not let your foot slip—
>   he who watches over you will not slumber;
> indeed, he who watches over Israel
>   will neither slumber nor sleep. (Psalm 121:3–4)

> And we know that in all things God works for the good of those who love him, who have been called according to his purpose. (Romans 8:28)

> Now to him who is able to do immeasurably more

than all we ask or imagine, according to his power
that is at work within us... (Ephesians 3:20)

Recently, I had my cup of learning from house fires "re-filled." On a Friday night when we had the grandchildren, we made the mistake of putting a pizza box in the fireplace where a gentle and relaxing fire was slowly burning.

In a matter of seconds the box was consumed by flames, and we heard what sounded like a train climbing up the chimney. I tried to be calm as I asked my husband if I should call the fire department. He surmised that things would calm right down after the box burned, but as the sound grew louder, the flames wilder and smoke started filling the room, he agreed we should call 911.

After calling, we quickly grabbed the sleeping children, the car keys and the dogs. It was bitterly cold outside so my husband started the car and put the dogs in while waiting for the fire truck to arrive. The children and I climbed into the other car, which unfortunately he had forgotten to start in all the chaos. (At least the dogs remained warm.)

Momentarily, firefighters clad in their heavy boots with axes perched over their shoulders stormed through our front door (and onto my newly shampooed carpets). Fortunately, they were able to contain the chimney fire without using the hoses or breaking through the roof. I was so grateful for those firefighters and gained a different spiritual lesson from this house fire.

Earlier I had realized how God was always at work; this time I began to think of the ways the Scriptures (and those who carry them) are like the firefighters. They have impact. Sometimes we feel like they barge in and disrupt our quiet evening; sometimes we feel like they "mess up" our neatly arranged house and shampooed carpet.

In this instance we were tempted to just try and "take care of things ourselves" and not call in reinforcement. I'm so thankful we did call for help and help arrived. The disruption was so trivial compared to the treasure of safety for our grandchildren.

In your cup of learning let the Bible speak to you and even disrupt your comfort and ease. The Scriptures are alive and active and are able to have a life-changing, life-saving effect on those they touch. However, we must call for them and let them rush into the front door of our heart. It could save our life, eternally. The lessons from house fires remind me to never underestimate the power of God's work and God's word:

> As the rain and the snow
>   come down from heaven,
> and do not return to it
>   without watering the earth
> and making it bud and flourish,
>   so that it yields seed for the sower and bread for

    the eater,
so is my word that goes out from my mouth:
    It will not return to me empty,
but will accomplish what I desire
    and achieve the purpose for which I sent it.
    (Isaiah 55:10–11)

For the word of God is living and active. Sharper than any double-edged sword, it penetrates even to dividing soul and spirit, joints and marrow; it judges the thoughts and attitudes of the heart. Nothing in all creation is hidden from God's sight. Everything is uncovered and laid bare before the eyes of him to whom we must give account. (Hebrews 4:12–13)

When You Are Caught in a Riot

Twice I have feared for my life while in the middle of a great commotion.

I was in high school in the South in the late 1960s and early 1970s. The schools where I lived had always been segregated, an apartheid of sorts. My high school senior year would be the vanguard of desegregation for my town where a large "black" and a large "white" high school would come together. Suffice it to say, the year was tumultuous.

Many days the National Guard was called to calm skirmishes that would erupt on the campus. The bathrooms were constantly locked. They were too dangerous to enter. We had to forego the usual school plays and activities of the year. Several times we went into what today is termed "lockdown" mode.

As a student body officer, I remember one day being in a student government meeting that was made up of students from both schools. Those meetings were seen as beneficial in bringing a more peaceful merger. To the best of my memory, they were often spirited but congenial.

After one of these meetings, I remember walking back to my classroom with others from the group. Before we could grasp what was happening, an angry mob of students was approaching us. It was frightening. There was no control as people were screaming and fists were flying. I remember my dress being torn and ripped partly off when one of my friends (thankfully, a strong male) stepped in, telling me to run as fast as I could, and I did—right to the safety of a classroom. Unfortunately the friend who helped me ended up in the emergency room with a broken nose.

The second experience happened much later in life when my daughter Melissa was in high school. We had gained deep convictions about serving the poor and had collected clothes to give away when we were at a conference in the Philippines. Smoky Mountain in Manila is a place I'll never forget. This "mountain" is made from tons and tons of garbage. People live on this trash heap in cardboard houses with dirt floors. Children play outside with whatever interesting bits of trash they can find.

This particular afternoon Melissa and I, along with our friend Roxanne, went to this slum to give away clothes to the children. They were thrilled; so much so that they all came out. Hundreds of mothers and fathers and children swarmed toward us, quickly closing in on where we were standing. Melissa fell down due to all the pushing and shoving that ensued and was in danger of being stampeded. The scene was heart-stoppingly frightening.

Roxanne reached Melissa before I could and pulled her away. We were still being pursued and began throwing the bags (suitcases and all) of clothing as far away from us as we could. This caused the mob to go in the direction of the bags. We ran as fast as we could back to safety.

The lesson I was tempted to take away was to (a) no longer try to help in unknown situations and (b) avoid masses of people while bearing gifts. Often, it seems that "getting your hands dirty" by helping others puts you in harm's way. Sometimes it can bring about physical danger, and at other times it can bring emotional pain.

I can think of several times, some not appropriate to write about, where trying to help others resulted in betrayal. I can begin to ask myself if it's worth it to keep trying to help when it's not appreciated or when it backfires.

I am often inspired by the poem "Anyway" penned on an orphanage wall in Albania by Mother Teresa, who adapted it from a Kent Keith poem. Scripture confirms its truth.

People are unreasonable,
illogical and self centered.
Love them anyway.

If you do good,
people will accuse you of selfish, ulterior motives.
Do good anyway.

If you are successful,
you win false friends and true enemies.
Succeed anyway.

The good you do will be forgotten tomorrow.
Do good anyway.

Honesty and frankness make you vulnerable.
Be honest and frank anyway.

What you spent years building
may be destroyed overnight.
Build anyway.

People really need help
but may attack you if you help them.
Help people anyway.

Give the world the best you have
and you'll get kicked in the teeth.
Give the world the best you've got anyway.

You see, in the final analysis,
it is between you and God.
It never was between you and them anyway.

In both of the scary situations I described, I was trying to do something positive to help other people. The following scripture is a great motivator for us to continue to do good to others:

> Let us not become weary in doing good, for at the proper time we will reap a harvest if we do not give up. Therefore, as we have opportunity, let us do good to all people, especially to those who belong to the family of believers. (Galatians 6:9–10)

This scripture is a short yet profound teaching from God. It instructs me to not become weary in doing good and to never give up. Even though the high-school mob did not appreciate what the other class officers and I were trying to do to make our school a fair and peaceful place, it was still right that I was trying. And with the situation on Smoky Mountain, I keep imagining how I might feel if I lived on the garbage dump and it was my child who needed clothes. Thinking these situations through helps me not grow weary.

I also think of and learn from the verses in 1 Peter 2:20–24:

> But how is it to your credit if you receive a beating for doing wrong and endure it? But if you suffer for doing good and you endure it, this is commendable

before God. To this you were called, because Christ suffered for you, leaving you an example, that you should follow in his steps.

"He committed no sin,
and no deceit was found in his mouth."

When they hurled their insults at him, he did not retaliate; when he suffered, he made no threats. Instead, he entrusted himself to him who judges justly. He himself bore our sins in his body on the tree, so that we might die to sins and live for righteousness; by his wounds you have been healed.

Sometimes when my efforts to serve go unnoticed, I am tempted to slack off or grow weary. I can be tempted to be resentful when service is not appreciated. Yet, Jesus' continual loving actions were often met with resistance and even hatred. He never quit giving or doing good. I have a long way to go to be like Jesus. The desire to be comfortable slips in so easily.

We are all called by God to keep on giving and keep on trying to make a difference in this world, even when it's hard and brings suffering. Jesus went first. He left footprints I can step in to follow. I need those tracks. They lead me to the right places. Without them, I can get weary and want to run the other way.

When You Have to Wait for Answers

Anyone who has had a sick child knows the heartache involved. I am inspired by so many women around the world who have responded with faith to very difficult and sometimes tragic circumstances involving their children. Often, we have to wait to find answers and solutions for their needs. At other times the answers we seek and long for are beyond our reach and our human understanding.

Our first child (Melissa) grew up with the typical ear infections, colds, childhood diseases and even a few broken bones and trips to the emergency room. Our second child (Kristen) had the same kinds of experiences until she was about eleven years old. At that point she was recovering from chickenpox, and was eager to be well and back to school.

The chickenpox ended, and then it seemed she began getting one illness after another. Often, she would be in extreme abdominal pain and would be vomiting throughout the night. She missed day after day of school. For the next three or four years, she missed over sixty days of school each year. When she was able to make it, she would often have to go in late or come home early.

This trying situation took a great toll on her confidence and on some of her friendships during that time. Friends in school understandably don't like to wait for you to feel better, and when you are out of touch, you also tend to be "out of mind."

Some teachers were fabulous in their understanding and compassion while others were completely difficult and without any sympathy. Somehow, through tutoring and hard work, she was able to keep up.

We went to doctor appointment after doctor appointment looking for answers. Too few took this seriously; some guessed; some wrote it off as a recurrent virus or an autoimmune disease of some kind. I knew as a mom this was not acceptable and something wasn't right. I did a great deal of research and sought much advice.

Kristen became very discouraged and was tempted to be angry with God for her malady. Each morning we would be hopeful that this would be the day when the pain and vomiting would subside...only to be disappointed again and again.

Most tests, which were often strenuous, were inconclusive. We were all tired of waiting. Often I would be filled with guilt and discouragement as I had to work out a difficult schedule of care for her between my husband's and my work and travel responsibilities, and the needs of the other children.

After tests, it often seemed the worst news was "no news." Even as I write this, I find myself sighing remembering how often hope would be deferred and disappointment would crowd in. We prayed and we cried. This went on for several years.

After changing doctors several times, I felt a new ray of hope when a new doctor was appalled that Kristen had not been admitted for a certain battery of tests. The doctor had a "fire in her eyes" and a determination to find answers. She referred her to Children's Hospital where she would see a pediatric gastroenterologist. I had been trying to get something like this to happen for such a long time. Frustrated, but grateful, we awaited the appointment.

After a few procedures, and because of the difficulty of one of them, the specialist was convinced he had found the problem. I won't try to describe it in detail, but there was an issue with her esophagus and her intestinal tract that had been previously undiscovered. He surmised that a certain and simple combination of treatments would resolve and alleviate the symptoms and prescribed two medicines for her.

After several years of near daily pain and vomiting, two days on this medicine resolved all of her symptoms! She had forgotten what it felt like to feel good and had a brand new lease on life.

After a couple of years of treatment with the medicine, she was weaned off and has been medicine-free and completely healthy since that time. She went on to graduate from high school and college, work in the ministry, get her master's degree, become a high school teacher, and then become a wife and mother.

I'm sure more than she wanted was poured into her cup of learning for those years. I know it was in mine. As I look back, I remember how many times we were faced with uncertainty, no answers and waiting. What do you do when those things are in your cup of learning?

I had to go to the Bible, pray, talk with others and wait...and wait...and wait. To my shame I don't enjoy waiting. I dislike lines; I get restless in traffic; I like my Internet modem to operate at lightning speed. Heaven forbid I get put on hold and have to wait to speak to someone who can help me resolve a problem! Then when we are connected I often don't understand his/her accent, and the frustration can mount. I like for pictures to be posted before the day of their taking is over. We live in an "instant" time where waiting is passé. Forced waiting, as in the situation with my daughter, has poured much into my cup of learning.

God's timetable is not the same as mine. Waiting is necessary for God's work to be done. Sometimes God has not completed the interweaving, and sometimes we need the waiting. Prematurity, whether in birth or character, is laden with difficulties.

> As you do not know the path of the wind,
>   or how the body is formed in a mother's womb,
> so you cannot understand the work of God,
>   the Maker of all things.
>
> Sow your seed in the morning,
>   and at evening let not your hands be idle,
> for you do not know which will succeed,
>   whether this or that,
> or whether both will do equally well.
> (Ecclesiastes 11:5–6)

While at times wondering if God heard me or really cared, I have been continually reminded of the importance of holding to the promise that he does in fact hear me and care for me. He has the power and the willingness to help me. Waiting is essential for my spiritual growth. It tests my faith and builds my character.

Several scriptures encourage me when I am in waiting mode:

Yet the LORD longs to be gracious to you;
    he rises to show you compassion.
For the LORD is a God of justice.
    Blessed are all who wait for him! (Isaiah 30:18)

But those who wait for the LORD shall renew their
        strength,
    they shall mount up with wings like eagles,
they shall run and not be weary,
    they shall walk and not faint. (Isaiah 40:31 NRSV)

I wait for the LORD, my soul waits,
    and in his word I put my hope. (Psalm 130:5)

Since ancient times no one has heard,
    no ear has perceived,
no eye has seen any God besides you,
    who acts on behalf of those who wait for him.
    (Isaiah 64:4)

When the Phone Rings Too Often

The first phone call came in the middle of our summer vacation. Wyndham's mother had passed away. It was a phone call that we knew would be coming soon, but still one of those you can never quite be ready to receive.

Over the next few years the phone kept ringing and ringing, showing the Florida area code "352." It was all bad news.

A year after Wyndham's mother died, I got the "352" call telling me I should get down to Florida right away, as my dad did not have long to live. I cried all the way down, remembering so many things I loved and appreciated about him. I treasure that I was able to be with him and my sisters as he breathed his last. I missed my dad greatly, but was happy that my mom was still so healthy and able to live well on her own.

Not much time had passed when I got the call that the "stomach virus" my mom had when I was visiting her a few months earlier was actually cancer. Surgery would soon follow. I got to be there for her surgery, but the news was not good. Cancer cells had spread, and she was given the prognosis of a year or two to live.

However, the next month, immediately after our son's wedding and during our family vacation, the phone rang again. I cringed when I saw the "352" area code. It seemed to bring bad news upon bad news. I would be making another sad trip…my mom had died. This happened much sooner than we had thought it would.

A little over a year later another phone call came with that area code, filling me immediately with dread. My niece and her boyfriend had just been killed in a tragic car accident. She left behind four young children, now parentless. My sister, who is older than I am, would need to raise two of them. (The other two had a different father, and they went with him.)

A few months later I felt sick to my stomach as I saw the familiar Florida area code call revealed as the phone rang early one morning. Once again I dreaded hearing what news would come from the other side of the line. That call let us know that Wyndham's only brother had died unexpectedly from a stroke following disc surgery on his back. He had recently been to our house to visit. It all seemed surreal.

Soon after this my sister called, this time to say she had just found out she had lung cancer. My grief felt too heavy to bear. However, soon a follow-up call sent the wonderful news that her surgery had shown she did not have cancer after all. She was, and is, healthy! A sense of relief washed over me.

Sometimes it seems bad news comes in waves. How do you even respond to difficult calls that tell you a loved one has passed away? The grief is so deep. My cup of learning was difficult to drink. Through these trying times several scriptures and lessons from God kept grounding me:

> Surely he will never be shaken;
>> a righteous man will be remembered forever.
> He will have no fear of bad news;
>> his heart is steadfast, trusting in the LORD.
> His heart is secure, he will have no fear;
>> in the end he will look in triumph on his foes.
>> (Psalm 112:6–8)

> My comfort in my suffering is this:
>> Your promise preserves my life. (Psalm 119:50)

> May your unfailing love be my comfort,
>> according to your promise to your servant.
>> (Psalm 119:76)

Praise be to the God and Father of our Lord Jesus Christ, the Father of compassion and the God of all comfort, who comforts us in all our troubles, so that we can comfort those in any trouble with the comfort we ourselves have received from God. For just as the sufferings of Christ flow over into our lives, so also through Christ our comfort overflows. (2 Corinthians 1:3–5)

I cannot imagine going through times of grief without the comfort of my God. I remembered asking a friend how her faith was doing after she had lost her young brother unexpectedly. She told me that many had asked her about her faith. She explained that it was times like these that her faith meant the most. This is when it became faith because she couldn't see the good at that time. She couldn't see past the pain. She simply had to trust God.

God never promises us that life will be easy. In fact, he promises that there will be suffering. This doesn't mean he is not loving or just. We live in a fallen world, and the absence of good (evil) is always around us, and so is pain. If I didn't feel pain in this world, I would not see my need for God. I know and appreciate more than ever that this life is fleeting and that eternal life with God is the only constant I can put my trust in.

God's truths point me to the perspective that outside of him, there really is no one who can fill my void. Jesus knows what it is to suffer, and he feels and hurts over our pain. God's promises are precious to me.

I also am learning the truth of the scripture above: God's comfort to me allows me to have something to give to others. Without being filled with God, I would simply have nothing to give.

His promises are never-ending and will not fail me. They help me drink the cup that my life brings me. I have everything I need to both drink that cup and to give to others who are drinking theirs.

God not only uses life situations to fill our cups of learning, but also uses people. While I have learned so much from countless women (and men), I have chosen in this book to mention three women who have helped me learn a great deal about God. I will share about them in the next three chapters.

When There Seems to Be No Hope

Ionela Testa

> "For I know the plans I have for you," declares the LORD, "plans to prosper you and not to harm you, plans to give you hope and a future."
>
> Jeremiah 29:11

Special events such as weddings happen with considerable consistency and are occasions of joy. There are also certain times in life that are epiphanies that bring greater meaning and understanding of the power and grace of God. They cause you to stand in awe of our mighty God as you watch the Scriptures unfold in people's lives before your very eyes.

A recent wedding was one of those days for me. It brought together years of tears, joys, deep relationships and the sacrifices of Christians from churches in Boston; New Hampshire; Chicago; and Bucharest, Romania.

The following scripture reminds me of how God worked in the life of Ionela, the beautiful bride:

> From one man he made every nation of men, that
> they should inhabit the whole earth; and he deter-
> mined the times set for them and the exact places
> where they should live. God did this so that men
> would seek him and perhaps reach out for him and
> find him, though he is not far from each one of us.
> (Acts 17:26–27)

Let me give you the background: One afternoon in early 1999 I received a call from Wyndham, who was in Romania at the time. We worked full-time with HOPE *worldwide*, an NGO dedicated to helping those in need, and were preparing to open the Center of Hope in Saftica, Romania, which is just outside of Bucharest. This would be a Christian-staffed home for up to fourteen orphans below the age of ten. The children had already been se-lected by the county from an orphanage, and their arrival date was set.

I had been making many trips to Romania, preparing for this center. And at one point Wyndham was there with-out me, doing some work for the home-to-be, as well as visiting the church in Bucharest.

Mr. Biris, an official who served as the director of child protection services for the county, was involved with us as we prepared to open the home. He asked Wyndham to make a visit with him. Mr. Biris took him down back roads and into an area of deep poverty. Upon arriving at their destination, Mr. Biris introduced Wyndham to three children, all siblings. Ionela was fifteen, Claudia was fourteen, and Alex was soon to be twelve. They were living in a tiny dark shack with no heat. They had been abandoned and were forced to leave their home for a number of reasons.

Life had been extremely difficult. Ionela worked hard to take care of and feed her siblings. The other two took on jobs too, and Ionela made sure they all rode the public transport over an hour each way to go to school. Their situation was desperate. Wyndham called me to let me know we needed to add these three older children to the home.

Back at the HOPE *worldwide* New England office, we reasoned that taking in older children could be detrimental to the younger children from the orphanage who were coming to the home. That is why we had settled on a younger age group for the home. We also knew we had already accepted more children than we felt we could adequately care for.

However, Wyndham persuaded us that this was a move that needed to happen, and with much prayer we trusted that the time and place of meeting these three children was no accident. We would take them in. Mr. Biris felt these older children could be an example for the others. Little did we know at the time how true his prediction would become.

Ionela, Claudia and Alex moved into the home, joining two children already there who had grown up in a Bucharest orphanage with our son Jacob, whom we had adopted in 1998. A doctor and her husband from the church in Boston, along with their new baby, were living there as house parents.

The day the three moved in was Alex's twelfth birthday, and we realized he had never had a birthday celebration. I remember Ionela's tears as he received a cake and birthday honoring; she was so thrilled for her brother. Ionela's and Claudia's next birthdays would also be the first birthday celebrations they had ever had.

The other twelve children from the orphanage arrived soon afterward. Their arrival and the ensuing chaos are forever stamped into my brain. I was there for the inaugural day, and I phoned home the next day telling Wyndham, "We may have made a grand mistake." (And understand, I am without doubt a "glass half full" person.)

I cannot even put into words the challenge of the first few days and weeks. Children were wailing through the night, literally climbing the walls and banging their heads against the floor.

The staff in the home became heroes to me. Meanwhile, Ionela and her siblings helped out, though also a bit overwhelmed by the challenge before us.

Several incidents that ensued nine or so months later are emblazoned in my mind's eye. I will never forget the joy of walking around the facility of the HOPE home in Saftica the summer after the children came. (We were there directing a HOPE Youth Corps in which teens from other places had come to serve the children and meet needs in the home.)

The picture below is of Ionela. I had come upon her in

a quiet corner of the yard early in the morning, entrenched in reading her Romanian Bible. No one had asked her to or expected it of her; she simply wanted to know about this God she was seeing in the lives of so many. She read and studied, and opened up her life with the disciples there. There are few joys that stand out to me more than the day she was baptized into Jesus. God smiled on me and allowed me to be there and help baptize her. I marveled at the way God was working as he searches the earth for hearts fully committed to him.

> At that time Hanani the seer came to Asa king of Judah and said to him: "Because you relied on the king of Aram and not on the LORD your God, the army of the king of Aram has escaped from your hand. Were not the Cushites and Libyans a mighty army with great numbers of chariots and horsemen? Yet when you relied on the LORD, he delivered them into your hand. *For the eyes of the LORD range throughout the earth to strengthen those whose hearts are fully committed to him.* (2 Chronicles 16:7–9, emphasis added)

So many of the children shared what Ionela meant to them as a big sister when we all sat around the living room right before she was baptized in the portable baptistry.

A New England friend of ours was very involved in the opening and advancement of the home. He made numerous trips to Romania in which he got to know the children and helped train the staff.

When he returned from one of those trips proposing the idea of adopting three teenagers to join their three young children, his wife thought he might be extremely jet-lagged. However, with great faith and the support of the church, they gave Ionela, Claudia and Alex a new home, a new family and new opportunities in New England.

Ionela graduated from high school. Claudia studied the Bible, made a decision to be a disciple of Jesus and was baptized. Ionela then went to University of New England and began a campus outreach along with a friend she had helped become a Christian while in high school.

She had participated in the HOPE Youth Corps in Chicago one summer during high school. There she had become friends with Anthony Testa, who was a disciple in the Chicago teen ministry and also on the Youth Corps. (Later Ionela would transfer to a college in DeKalb, Illinois.)

Now, back to that special wedding I began the chapter talking about: On a beautiful Saturday afternoon as the Rascal Flatts' tune rang out in the church, "God Blessed the Broken Road That Led Me Straight to You," Ionela walked down the aisle holding the arm of her dad to marry Anthony.

Together they serve on the Chicago Church staff in the DeKalb campus ministry. Ionela is one of the brightest, boldest, most well-spoken shining stars for Jesus I have had the privilege to know.

Ionela's broken road has had many very difficult twists and turns and has taken her quite a distance from that dark, cold room in Romania where we first came to know her. God certainly did bless the broken road that led her straight to him. And in so doing, he inspired many through her courageous, faith-filled journey down that road. God can do the impossible, and touch and use our lives in ways that we can't even imagine.

> Now to him who is able to do immeasurably more than all we ask or imagine, according to his power that is at work within us, to him be glory in the church and in Christ Jesus throughout all generations, for ever and ever! Amen. (Ephesians 3:20–21)

When Everything Goes Wrong

Elise Daigle

As I sat in the salon awaiting my haircut, my hair-dresser scurried to retrieve a book she was eager to show me. This woman devotes her day off each week to style and cut hair for anyone who has lost their job. She charges nothing, only asks that they "pay it forward" by showing generosity and kindness to someone else. This simple gesture of kindness has brought her national attention, as well as several journal books filled with thank-you messages and descriptions of ways this act has impacted women all over the world. As her clients read these journals, they are often moved to help as well.

As I received the journal she said to me, "You have to read this!"

She said she had been more impacted by this woman than any other. As I glanced down at the entry, I exclaimed, "Oh, these are my friends! We go to church together."

The writing was a message of thanks and a brief-as-possible explanation as to why Elise was unemployed. Her words were transcribed by Ellen Faller, who had brought her to the hair salon. Elise has for now lost most of her vision and ability to put her words on paper.

As I got the opportunity to sit with Elise and talk with her recently about her life, I felt it would be selfish not to share at least a portion of her story of faith and perseverance with you. Some of her story I had heard and witnessed. Much I had not. It was hard to listen to all that has happened to her. I can't imagine having lived this story. As I listened and asked questions, two scriptures came to mind. This is the first one:

> "For my thoughts are not your thoughts,
>   neither are your ways my ways,"
>   declares the Lord.
> "As the heavens are higher than the earth,
>   so are my ways higher than your ways
>   and my thoughts than your thoughts.
> As the rain and the snow
>   come down from heaven,
> and do not return to it
>   without watering the earth
> and making it bud and flourish,
>   so that it yields seed for the sower and bread for
>   the eater,
> so is my word that goes out from my mouth:
>   It will not return to me empty,
> but will accomplish what I desire
>   and achieve the purpose for which I sent it."
>   (Isaiah 55:8–11)

I cannot understand and know why some people have to experience such hardships. I don't have to understand now, as God is bigger than I and God is good. As with Job, certainly God and Satan are both active. God can have great confidence in some people to weather tremendous attacks of Satan, and Satan is always on the prowl. Satan seeks to destroy. God will ultimately bless a hundredfold— if not in this lifetime, in our eternal home. This brings to mind the second scripture:

> I consider that our present sufferings are not worth comparing with the glory that will be revealed in us. (Romans 8:18)

Whatever we go through here will one day seem light and momentary in comparison to what God has prepared for us.

As a young bride, bright and visionary, Elise had many dreams before her. God had already spared her life once: When she was sixteen, she had been diagnosed with cancer. Thankfully, she was treated and cured.

Nine days after her wedding her new husband was killed in a tragic automobile crash, as a tractor trailer fell off a bridge onto his car.

She later married a man who was kind, and yet hardships awaited again. After losing twins and another child born prematurely, they parted ways—his alternative lifestyle drew him away.

She married again. This marriage was also filled with great difficulty, which I will not describe. However, during this time she was blessed with two beautiful daughters, both now in college. The doctors had advised her to abort the second daughter, saying she would be born with severe brain and heart damage. (She is a bright, healthy young woman.)

Soon Elise developed her second cancer, resulting in a hysterectomy, but which was also considered cured. Later she developed breast cancer, which was treated successfully.

Elise has always had a heart to give and make a difference in this world. As a nurse, she began a very successful business in which she worked with terminally ill children, trying to make their end on this earth as pleasant as possible. Many of the incidents she shares from her life during this time are not only touching, but faith-building. She did this type of work because she was gifted in this area and wanted to contribute in a way that could make a difference in the lives not just of the children, but of their families.

In 1998 her neighbors, Kevin and Debbie McDaniel, reached out to her and she became a disciple of Jesus. She was filled with deep convictions and passionate love for the Lord.

Not long after becoming a Christian, she was doing a routine errand in a nice suburban area after joining her church family group for a movie. Dragged from the parking lot, she fell victim to a horrifically violent crime and was left for dead. Found by the store clerk who saw her papers scattered near her car, she was taken to the hospital. Though the trauma was severe, she recovered—thanks to the power of God and support of her brothers and sisters. She continued to give and to serve others.

Involved as a trainer of foster parents for the Department of Social Services in addition to her nursing job, she became aware of the dire needs of an infant and toddler who were distant relatives of hers. For two years she took them into her home and cared for them. Elise takes the example and teaching of Jesus to heart as he calls us to "love our neighbors as ourselves."

She soon developed an aggressive breast cancer. She was preparing for a double mastectomy a few months ago as she went to the hospital for an MRI. During this procedure, it became apparent she was extremely allergic to the dye, and she went into a severe reaction. She was treated with a drug to which she was also allergic.

Nearing death, her heart rate rose to over three hundred beats a minute for an extended time. As a result she had a severe brain aneurysm. Over 75% of those with this malady never make it to the operating table. Of the 25% who survive and have the surgery, half don't make it through.

As prayers and fasting went forth for her, God chose to have her beat the odds and make it through the surgery. I remember speaking to one of the nurses immediately after the surgery who said she could not be given what was needed afterward because of her allergies and that a stroke was likely imminent.

After she survived the surgery, the doctor came to her room to tell her she would never talk or walk again. She looked at him and asked him to leave her room. Shocked, he said, "Did you say something?" to which she replied, "Yes. Please leave my room." She would not tolerate faithlessness in what she was confident would happen in her life as she continued to make a difference in others' lives.

Elise has been talking since and has much to say. Even as I was hearing her more complete story, God was the focus. No matter what is happening to her, somehow Elise will figure out some way to serve you. This is inspiring, yet humbling. She is convinced she will recover. The aneurysm left her nearly blind, deaf in one ear, unable to put her words on paper. Nausea is a constant companion. She has lost feeling in a leg, so she gets around with a walker.

Each morning she must wrap one arm (to keep down the swelling from lymphedema) and wrap her abdomen (to allow more blood flow to her brain to keep her from passing out). She then puts on a prosthetic leg piece to help her mobility with the leg she cannot feel. Her needed mastectomy has to be postponed indefinitely as she recovers.

I am humbled with the attitude that Elise displays. She harbors no bitterness or self-pity. She is all about loving God and others. Convinced God wants her alive for a reason, she is eager to live out her days serving him. She is headed "true north."

I am also inspired as I watch her family group from church surround her. When you see Elise, certainly Maureen or Ellen and others will not be far away. These women know what "family group" really means. This is truly the kind of familial devotion that must have been at the heart of Jesus' words recorded in Mark 10:

> Jesus looked at them and said, "With man this is impossible, but not with God; all things are possible with God."
>
> Peter said to him, "We have left everything to follow you!"
>
> "I tell you the truth," Jesus replied, "no one who has left home or brothers or sisters or mother or father or children or fields for me and the gospel will fail to

> receive a hundred times as much in this present age
> (homes, brothers, sisters, mothers, children and
> fields—and with them, persecutions) and in the age
> to come, eternal life. But many who are first will be
> last, and the last first." (Mark 10:27–31)

As you read this, please pray for her and for God to use her life in many ways.

After writing the previous part of this chapter, enough time has passed for me to have an update on Elise. I want to share this with you. She is making progress from the brain surgery. She can walk with a walker and read one word at a time by using a magnifying bookmark with a hole cut out for each word. Processing is difficult. The day before some of us went to pray with her, she was (with her walker and her bound arm) making dinner for her brother and also for the family of someone in the church who had just lost his father. Also, she had prepared tea and coffee cake for us.

A few days prior I hosted a baby shower for a friend who was adopting a baby. That morning the weather was terrible—a New England nor'easter. Elise had a friend pick her up and was the first one there.

Later in the afternoon after the shower, the church was having a large Christmas celebration. Usually Elise is at church each week though sometimes the singing will send her into a seizure. The music at the Christmas event would be more than her brain could process. So instead of attending, she took her little bookmark with the hole cut out and eagerly read the entire book of Job, word by word. It took her six hours.

After undergoing a radical mastectomy to remove the aggressive cancer, her attitude was one of excitement and gratitude that she was "well enough to have surgery."

While many would have retreated and become bitter or withdrawn, Elise serves. I am both convicted and inspired by her life. Her Job-like life has taught her and she has not wasted the lessons. They have made her, through her weaknesses, a stronger person. I pray that life's hard lessons may make us all stronger and more faithful, persevering and filled with the unconditional love of Jesus.

When Life Changes in an Instant

Peggy Malutinok

Peggy Malutinok's life changed in an instant two years ago. Her son Scott, who was a strong, fun and spiritual young man, had a horrific motorcycle accident that left him in a coma for weeks. He suffered severe brain damage. The Scott that Peggy had known and raised is no longer there. She has a different son in the same body.

Through Peggy I have come to appreciate the ways God uses the weak to teach us all about love and sacrifice. Peggy is an inspiration in her attitude and actions as she has sought to honor God and learn from him each day. I asked her to share some of the contents of her morning cups of learning. Thank you, Peggy.

Two years ago I was headed alone to the crash scene, knowing that the sirens surrounding me were headed toward my son Scott. Thanks be to God, suffering much bodily injury as well as severe brain trauma, Scott survived an accident that was marked on police reports as a "fatality." He has had to re-learn to walk, to speak, and to use practically every muscle in his body. He is also re-learning "executive" mental functions such as remembering words, names and events as well as navigating and planning.

Scott has come so very far. He loves nature and animals. So this fall he will most likely enter vocational training to either do landscaping or work with animals. Hopefully his memory will continue to grow, thus increasing his independence. He is consistently happy, respectful, spiritual, patient with rehabilitation, a willing student and fun-loving—qualities that are rare after suffering a brain injury.

As I look back, it is hard to believe the intensity of the last two years: the trials, the joys, and the ways that God has powerfully made his presence known.

We each have a unique race to run, and I write this for anyone who can use encouragement. One of the most helpful concepts these last two years has been that amid many things that I had no control over, *I always had choices*. In an effort to be brief I have included only a few of the hundreds of examples. The following choices have been so instrumental in navigating this challenging time.

Listen for God's Voice

As a self-reliant doer and fixer I am used to hearing my own voice more than any other, especially when I am not in over my head. This situation I could not fix. En route to the crash scene I prayed, "God, please let him live!"

I heard God quietly answer, "If he doesn't, he will be with me," which gave me much peace and perspective.

I've asked God, "What if he isn't able to walk? Will I ever hear his voice? See a smile?" Too many times to count I have heard God's answer. He has been beside me constantly through pain, worry, disappointments, decisions and frustrations—sometimes through a gentle voice, a scripture that would come to my mind, or a reminder of his love and power would be exhibited through his gifts of a fresh breeze and the beauty of nature.

When I chose to listen for his voice, I was much more surrendered and at peace, and I was able to find many ideas and solutions.

See God Working

I will never know exactly why the accident happened, but God lovingly cushioned so many of the struggles in ways I would not have noticed had I not been looking. Receiving news of the accident from a church friend who "happened" to be near the scene rather than the police, and six weeks later hearing Scott speak his first words to me on Mother's Day are only two of the many times I could feel God intervening on my behalf.

Envision My 'Set Point'

Somehow, goals center me, even in tragedy and especially dealing with something new or different. I knew quickly how I wanted to look back and see myself during this time—calm, solution-oriented and with a spiritual perspective regardless of circumstances and outcome. Of course I haven't always stayed on course, but having these qualities as a focus has given me a guide to get back to where I want to be.

Early on when asked Scott's prognosis, my answer (to myself and others) was, "Whatever happens, I know that God will give us the strength to make it through," and amid even current unknowns, that focus has been invaluable to me.

Focus on God's Word

Either God's words are true or they are not. Over thirty years ago I made the decision to accept them as truth (even the difficult ones). I have derived so much comfort, advice, inspiration and instruction from the Scriptures. Some familiar ones came automatically to mind, and I was excited to find many more that gave me peace and perspective.

From the first days after the accident until now I daily read three to four passages and choose one to "claim" for the day. Some of my favorites have been Psalm 18; Proverbs 31; Isaiah 40; Matthew 6:27; Ephesians 6:11; Romans 8:28, 37–39; Hebrews 10:39, 11:1.

After Scott was discharged from the rehabilitation unit and put solely in our care, I often told God (and still sometimes do), "I am *not* trained for this!"—to which the Scriptures calmly replied, "My grace is sufficient for you" (2 Corinthians 12:9).

I have also found many inspirational books which have been helpful and fresh to me. I am still moved to see the twenty-third psalm ("Even though I walk through the valley of the shadow of death, I will fear no evil.") posted in Scott's bedroom. This is one of the passages he had copied and posted on his wall before the accident!

Be Positive

Every morning as I woke up with a pit in my stomach and every night as I fell into bed exhausted, I knew that I could choose to focus on the often heartbreaking scenes of the day or on the encouraging ones. Some of my most precious memories have been seeing Scott nuzzling into his dad's neck, clinging for dear life to a stuffed animal that his sister Joyanna brought him, haltingly telling his brother John that "if you…could be…my brother…that would be *so* awesome!" and breaking his hunger strike only for his sister-in-law Shannen.

Other joyful memories have been of Scott learning to read again with the help of Nana, playing his first basketball games with Uncle Greg, having wheelchair races with Granny Olga, and clearly recognizing and enjoying the company of Uncle Paul's family even though names were not easily coming to mind.

Accept Help

In the brain injury community, recovery is termed "a marathon rather than a sprint," and each act, even from those unknown, has felt like a sprinkler or a cup of water offered as we've run this marathon. Thousands of prayers, cards, letters, posters; fifty loving friends crowding with our family into the hospital waiting room; the arrival of out-of-town family and friends dropping everything to offer encouragement and help; the teen ministry in Boston sending us videos to help jog Scott's memory; a group of Scott's friends that continues to spend one evening a week with him; hundreds of meals, rides, family and household needs met through our loving North River church family.

As our family waited for hours in the waiting room, it was so encouraging to gather around Facebook and Carepages to read messages and prayers coming in from around the world. The many, many of acts of love and service our family has been given have been humbling, but so refreshing. Had we chosen not to accept them or not to make our needs known, life would have been much harder and not nearly so encouraging.

Accept Myself and Others

I've had some bad days and still do. My husband, Dave, and I smile when we realize that rarely do we have a bad day on the same day. Scott sometimes has "off" days. Others don't always know how to help and have their own lives to live. I have learned (again!) that I can't always do and be my best, but that I can always recover and restart. Overall, it has helped me to accept that we all are new at navigating these waters, and that "Amazing Grace" is not something to be offered only at salvation!

Refresh Myself

This is one of my favorite choices! I sometimes have to make an effort when I don't feel like it, but when I involve myself in favorite hobbies, a funny movie, a quiet evening, a solo getaway, or even planning something fun to do for someone, it refreshes me for the harder times. I try to add simple treats and humor into each day, but also need several hours of free time weekly, as well as getting away with Dave or a friend for a few days every few months.

Home-schooling (or "mom school") has its advantages. Over the past eighteen months, Scott and I have enjoyed museums, parks, zoos, Frisbee, ping pong, basketball, road trips, beaches, visits to our beloved Boston, many movies, hikes, tennis, soccer, even passing football!

No, I haven't become a bodybuilder like Scott. Our treats also have included several trips to Chili's for the hot brownie slathered with ice cream and hot fudge sauce, and no movie gets seen without (butterless) popcorn.

Let the Important Be Important

Scott is continuing to improve, and his life (and consequently mine) has grown much richer in simplicity. Though he often cannot remember what he has read, he faithfully reads his Bible and prays in his room every morning before hitting the shower.

Finding sand dollars on the beach last summer, Scott happily gave each to a young boy close by. The mother was very touched. As she thanked him, Scott replied, "I'm just doing what I was born to do: to help people be happy."

Because of short-term memory issues, Scott is not currently able to work or to attend classes, so I am his primary teacher and life coach. As we go to the library, on field trips, run errands, or go to the gym or park, we often stop tō talk to others, to laugh at children, to admire clouds, to enjoy whatever is at hand—as well as look for needs that we can meet along the way.

Realize I Am Chosen

The Bible says that we each are created to do God's work (Ephesians 2:10). I believe that my best works lie in the talents, passions and interests God has given me, as well as the trials. Through necessity, I have read many books, spent many hundreds of hours creating curriculum, attending appointments, quizzing professionals and doing research. I can't say that I would voluntarily choose the events of the past two years, but through them I have met hundreds of hurting people whose language I now can somewhat speak: people in emergency rooms, hospitals, rehabilitation units, camps, schools and in a brain-injured community I knew nothing about. For a long time, my passion has been serving those with "special needs," and God has equipped me in heart and knowledge even further to do so.

A quote which has inspired me the past year (author unknown) states that our memories should never be bigger than our dreams. The apostle Paul also emphasizes this concept, admonishing us about "forgetting what is behind and straining toward what is ahead" (Philippians 3:13). I treasure the memories of life before Scott's accident, and sometimes I am still shocked to be part of the brain-injured world. Yet through the above choices, God has given me a strength, joy and focus I could never have imagined; a family who has been stretched but is stronger and closer than ever; and many new and exciting dreams.

I pray that you too may run your race experiencing God's strength and blessings.

The poem below describes the life I see Peggy living.

A Strong Woman Versus a Woman of Strength
(Revised from a poem by Luke Easter with Dee Cheeks)

A strong woman works out every day to keep her body in shape.
But a woman of strength kneels in prayer to keep her soul in shape.

A strong woman isn't afraid of anything.
But a woman of strength shows courage in the midst of her fear.

A strong woman won't let anyone get the best of
her.
But a woman of strength gives the best of her to
everyone.

A strong woman makes mistakes and avoids the
same in the future.
A woman of strength realizes life's mistakes can
also be God's blessings and capitalizes on them.

A strong woman walks sure-footedly.
But a woman of strength knows God will catch her
when she falls.

A strong woman wears the look of confidence on
her face.
But a woman of strength wears grace.

A strong woman has faith that she is strong enough
for the journey.
But a woman of strength has faith that it is in the
journey that she will become strong.

When Children Speak

Then little children were brought to Jesus for him to place his hands on them and pray for them. But the disciples rebuked those who brought them.

Jesus said, "Let the little children come to me, and do not hinder them, for the kingdom of heaven belongs to such as these."

Matthew 19:13–14

Another favorite "school of learning" I attend is filled with children. Jesus wanted us to be around children for a reason. They need us, but we also need them! Get to know the children around you and learn from them. As you teach children in classes or walk with them to view nature, be amazed at their insights into God. Sometimes I think because they are so newly from God, they have these special spiritual vistas. They haven't been hardened and confused by the thinking of the world.

The following excerpts are from some of the cups of learning I received from my grandchildren over a two-month period. I could write many more, but hopefully from these examples you can let children offer you their cups of learning. I've entitled these "Friday Night Delights," in honor of "Nana and Papa night."

January 31, 2009—I learn much about God through my grandchildren. Friday is my favorite night of the week. Wyndham (Papa) and I (Nana) keep our grandchildren while their parents teach at the campus devotional in downtown Boston. I don't do much work during this time; I just enjoy the relationship.

Throughout the day I think about how to make the time special. Each week we order pepperoni pizza, make brownies, play, watch an episode or two of Caillou and then put them to bed.

The making of the brownies has become a particularly favorite tradition. Together Emma and Caleb carefully put the brownie mix into the bowl. Caleb (three) puts the water in the bowl and Emma (six) adds the oil. Each one helps crack an egg, and as I add the eggs they always say, "Oh…baby chicks in there" or "Don't kill the egg!" Then we stir the batter.

I have come to understand that they love the brownie batter even more than the brownies. I thought it would be a fun and educational thing to teach Caleb to count to fifty as we stir the batter. (As their Nana, I let them dig their spoons into the bowl to retrieve generous gobs of chocolate goo.) I wanted to see if Caleb could finish the count to fifty so I slowed with anticipation to the finishing count…46…47…48…49…and…Caleb then yelled out with great excitement toward the final number…"Lick the bowl!"

The stirring part of this task is the "hard work." However, they are eager to get to the "final count" because then they can enjoy the fruit of their labor. Likewise, I need to look at the hard work part of my life as a joy because of what I'm working toward.

> Not that I have already obtained all this, or have already been made perfect, but I press on to take hold of that for which Christ Jesus took hold of me. Brothers, I do not consider myself yet to have taken hold of it. But one thing I do: Forgetting what is behind and straining toward what is ahead, I press on toward the goal to win the prize for which God has called me heavenward in Christ Jesus. (Philippians 3:12–14)

February 7, 2009—Poor little Caleb came in with goopy eyes and announced, "I have junctitis" (his pronunciation of an eye infection called conjunctivitis). He had been instructed to not hug anyone or get too close. This was tough for Emma and Caleb. It was difficult for them to avoid expressing their affection for one another.

As Caleb and I were working in the kitchen, he looked at me and said, "Nana, I love 'Deety' [an affectionate term

that stuck from an early version of his effort to say 'sister'].
God gave me such a wonderful sister."

In the other room Emma was with Papa. At the same
time she was expressing similar feelings for her brother.
She looked at Papa and said, "I want to hug Caleb so much
I'm going to have a love explosion!"

I can become dull in expression of my love for God to
those around me, assuming that they know it. Real love
must be expressed. When it comes from within, I just can't
hold it in.

> But if I say, "I will not mention him
>   or speak any more in his name,"
> his word is in my heart like a fire,
>   a fire shut up in my bones.
> I am weary of holding it in;
>   indeed, I cannot. (Jeremiah 20:9)

Jeremiah and Caleb would admonish us: Have a love
explosion!

February 14, 2009—My Valentine, Wyndham, was thousands of miles away in Estonia this Friday evening. I
looked forward to the time with the kids. After Melissa
pulled into our driveway, Emma eagerly jumped out of the
car and ran into the house. She was so excited as she thrust
a handmade valentine into my hand. It was carefully cut
into a heart shape with a colorful "Emma original" drawing

of Nana and Emma standing together with the words, "I love you Nana."

The valentine is a treasure, now mounted on the refrigerator. What makes it so special is, of course, the love and effort that went into it and her excitement in sharing it.

When I care about someone, I can't help but put effort into letting them know through words and actions! This is also the heart of Paul toward his friends in Thessalonica:

> We loved you so much that we were delighted to share with you not only the gospel of God but our lives as well, because you had become so dear to us.
> (1 Thessalonians 2:8)

February 21, 2009—Caleb loves everything about "Star Wars." I was delighted to have found a YouTube song earlier in the afternoon that I knew he would thoroughly enjoy. And he did. He watched it about five times. As we stood there together, he planted a kiss on my cheek, hugged me and said, "I love you, Nana."

The pizza and brownies were eaten and it was nearing bedtime. It was quite cool outside and a nice fire was ensuring a relaxing atmosphere for all. As we watched Caillou, he wanted to sit on my lap (well, I suggested it). As we were sitting there, he put his little bare foot on mine. It was a chilly night. He looked up at me and said, "Nana, you are so warm."

I just smiled, and the following scripture came to mind:

> As Jesus and his disciples were on their way, he came to a village where a woman named Martha opened her home to him. She had a sister called Mary, who sat at the Lord's feet listening to what he said. But Martha was distracted by all the preparations that had to be made. She came to him and asked, "Lord, don't you care that my sister has left me to do the work by myself? Tell her to help me!"
>
> "Martha, Martha," the Lord answered, "you are worried and upset about many things, but only one thing is needed. Mary has chosen what is better, and it will not be taken away from her." (Luke 10:38–42)

I reflected on my relationship with God and how I need to "be still, and know that He is God." He longs to hear me express love to him and notice things about him that touch me. I want to learn along with Martha that the presence of Jesus and my relationship with him is more important that all the many activities that surround serving him.

February 28, 2009—You know by now we always make brownies. So, I had cashed in on a deal at the grocery store last week. Ten boxes of brownie mix for ten dollars. It was also the store brand that I usually like. I bought two boxes. The brownie batter had been carefully stirred and it was time to lick the bowl. Emma and Caleb eagerly dug their spoons in and raised them to their mouths. When they tasted their spoonfuls, they began to gag and say, "Yechh! This is bad!" and pushed the bowl away.

Wondering what on earth could be the problem, I put my spoon in and had a taste. I then understood why these boxes were selling at such a bargain. Something was amiss in the ingredients; it tasted like there was a cup of salt in the batter. Foolishly hoping for the best, I decided to go ahead and cook them, thinking the bad flavor might cook away.

So, we waited and waited, eager to perform the second "taste test." This test resulted in another "yechh!!" The whole batch went in the trash, and we had to switch our dessert to chocolate pudding.

Purity of ingredients is a must for any recipe. If the ingredients for the brownies are messed up, the brownies won't turn out the way they are supposed to no matter how carefully or long they are baked.

Likewise, no matter how hard I try to make things in my life work, I will find the end result being "yechh…this isn't right" if I don't use the correct ingredients from the scriptures.

> But as for you, continue in what you have learned
> and have become convinced of, because you know

> those from whom you learned it, and how from infancy you have known the holy Scriptures, which are able to make you wise for salvation through faith in Christ Jesus. All Scripture is God-breathed and is useful for teaching, rebuking, correcting and training in righteousness, so that the man of God may be thoroughly equipped for every good work. (2 Timothy 3:14–17)

March 6, 2009—When Emma goes to sleep, she sleeps like the proverbial log. Once she's out, it's hard to wake her. She can fall asleep in a moment, so when it's bedtime we let her fall asleep downstairs in the living room with us. The pattern is set. Papa relaxes a bit on the sofa. Emma snuggles on the sofa next to Papa where she falls sound asleep in his arm. He loves this and loves looking at her saying, "This is my little 'punkin.'"

His arm often becomes painful in this position, but he doesn't want to move her because he so enjoys the special time. She falls off to sleep, secure as can be. He dutifully and adoringly lets her doze, tucked within his arm.

It's easy to fall asleep when we are in the arms of someone whose love we trust. Peacefulness becomes reality when we truly rest in the arms of our adoring Father who loves to hold us.

> On my bed I remember you;
>> I think of you through the watches of the night.

Because you are my help,
   I sing in the shadow of your wings.
My soul clings to you;
   your right hand upholds me. (Psalm 63:6–8)

March 7, 2009—The grandkids slept over at our house while their mom and dad attended a marriage retreat. My daughter Kristen and her husband came to pick them up the next morning. Caleb woke up eagerly anticipating the arrival of his beloved "Uncle Gus." He, with the help of his sister, had drawn a picture of Darth Vader (from *Star Wars*) that he could scarcely wait to give to him.

When Uncle Gus and Aunt Kristen arrived, both kids let out screams of joy. Caleb immediately ran to get his prized recently crafted picture and proudly handed it over to Uncle Gus exclaiming, "This is for you! Deety did most of it, and I did all of it!"

When we give something from ourselves to others, it feels good, right and enjoyable. However, sometimes it's easy to forget we couldn't give anything on our own. Like Caleb, we often want to claim credit for our "good deeds." In reality, every good gift we have to give comes from God. And God, who gives freely, allows us to feel the joy of giving.

Don't be deceived, my dear brothers. Every good and perfect gift is from above, coming down from

> the Father of the heavenly lights, who does not
> change like shifting shadows. (James 1:16–17)

March 13, 2009—Tonight both the kids were recovering from strep throat. They were feeling okay as they had just completed their medication. Emma came in stating, "Yay!! No more yucky medicine. I'm done!" Caleb quickly looked at me and sighed, "I wish it [the medicine] would never end." They had the same medicine. One hated it and one never wanted it to end. Yet they both had to take it. (Two days later they would have to repeat the process with stronger medicine as they quickly relapsed.)

God gives us what we need for our spiritual health and growth. Sometimes God's medicine for this growth is distasteful to us, and sometimes it tastes good. Sometimes we need more than one dose. To be spiritually healthy we need God's prescription for our lives no matter how it "tastes" for as long as we need to take it. The end result is always for our good.

> No discipline seems pleasant at the time, but painful.
> Later on, however, it produces a harvest of righteous-
> ness and peace for those who have been trained by
> it. (Hebrews 12:11)

March 20, 2009—Tonight the kids came, still on their medicine but feeling fine. We had fun doing the Friday night routines. Papa has strep throat tonight. (Go figure.) The kids were playing around, and Papa was in the office finishing up the taxes, so he was less available than usual.

Toward the end of the evening he came in to play and joked around with the kids saying, "Hey, where've you been? I haven't gotten much attention tonight, and I'm even sharing strep throat with you!"

Emma, not missing a beat, said, "Papa, that's because you've been busy and haven't given us any attention!"

Wanting more attention from God, we sometimes wonder where he is. We have not realized that all the while, we are the ones who have not drawn close to him.

> Look to the LORD and his strength;
>   seek his face always. (1 Chronicles 16:11)

> He went out to meet Asa and said to him, "Listen to me, Asa and all Judah and Benjamin. The LORD is with you when you are with him. If you seek him, he will be found by you, but if you forsake him, he will forsake you. (2 Chronicles 15:2)

> God did this so that men would seek him and perhaps reach out for him and find him, though he is not far from each one of us. (Acts 17:27)

March 27, 2009—Caleb came over where I was sitting while writing an e-mail. My computer reminded him of the *Star Wars* song I had shown him several weeks earlier. He sat beside me in the chair and asked if I'd show him the song again. I assured him I would after I finished my e-mail.

"What's an e-mail, Nana?" he asked.

I explained and he then said, "Are you finished? Can I see it now?"

Another second went by and he again asked, "Are you finished? Can I see it now?"...another second, "How 'bout now, Nana?" This was repeated about sixteen times, and I decided it was time to just stop what I was doing and give in. (This is a grandmother's prerogative.) After all, it is Friday night and he made clear his request. He got my attention.

Though God is never too busy for us, sometimes he may wonder just how important something is to us by the consistency with which we speak to him about it.

> Then Jesus told his disciples a parable to show them that they should always pray and not give up. He said: "In a certain town there was a judge who neither feared God nor cared about men. And there was a widow in that town who kept coming to him with the plea, 'Grant me justice against my adversary.'
>
> "For some time he refused. But finally he said to himself, 'Even though I don't fear God or care about men, yet because this widow keeps bothering me, I

will see that she gets justice, so that she won't eventually wear me out with her coming!'"

And the Lord said, "Listen to what the unjust judge says. And will not God bring about justice for his chosen ones, who cry out to him day and night? Will he keep putting them off? I tell you, he will see that they get justice, and quickly. However, when the Son of Man comes, will he find faith on the earth?" (Luke 18:1–8)

Persistence in our request shows how much something matters to us. If we don't keep asking, it is often either because it is not that important to us or because we don't believe God is listening. In reality, a grandparent's love can't even compare to God's love, care and concern for us.

When You Sit in the Backyard

Our small front yard overlooks a town park with a soccer field, tennis courts, softball field and playground. It was fun when the kids were growing up and is still a wonderful place to run the dogs and to meet people. However, since we have a very active recreation director in our town, the park has become extremely busy.

School buses often fill our street, and hundreds of people fill the park every spring, summer and fall day. High school soccer and tennis matches are played there as well as softball games. Traffic is heavy and everything has become loud! A backyard was starting to seem like a good idea, but we didn't have one. All we had were many trees overlooking the swampy earth below.

I have been influenced for many years by a small sign that was on my dad's desk at his workplace. It was the one belonging of his that I wanted to keep when he passed on. The little sign reads, "Now tell me all the ways it can be done!"

This little sentence is based on a biblical principle and

reflects the faithful attitude of Joshua and Caleb. What if God had seen our messy lives and said, "Too bad for them. I can't fix that!" He had a plan for our redemption because of his love and his ability to do anything. After all, he spoke the world into existence. He specializes in making something from nothing.

So, with this "tell me how it can be done" outlook, we looked for a way to have a backyard. It became clear that it would take research, hard work and money to transform a small forest to a true backyard. God sees beyond the human eye with his vision. If I let what I see in front of me stop me from dreaming, I am not imitating God's attributes.

I'm inspired and challenged by Paul's account of Abraham.

> Therefore, the promise comes by faith, so that it may be by grace and may be guaranteed to all Abraham's offspring—not only to those who are of the law but also to those who are of the faith of Abraham. He is the father of us all. As it is written: "I have made you a father of many nations." He is our father in the sight of God, in whom he believed—the God who gives life to the dead and calls things that are not as though they were.
>
> Against all hope, Abraham in hope believed and so became the father of many nations, just as it had been said to him, "So shall your offspring be." Without

weakening in his faith, he faced the fact that his body was as good as dead—since he was about a hundred years old—and that Sarah's womb was also dead. Yet he did not waver through unbelief regarding the promise of God, but was strengthened in his faith and gave glory to God. (Romans 4:16–20)

We needed to "call things that are not as though they were"; that is, we needed to call our small forest a backyard even though it wasn't…yet!

The first task to make our backyard would be to remove the obstacles—in this case about twenty large trees. Spiritually the same thing happens. In order to build, in order to move forward in our lives we have to remove all obstacles. Sometimes they have deep roots and have to be taken down with a chainsaw (so to speak) and a shovel.

Sometimes we find challenges in our life that we cannot move, and so we have to reassess our plans. Once the trees came down and the stumps were dug out, we still had an obstacle. It was in the form of a giant rock (about ten feet in diameter), steadfast and immovable. We wisely decided to incorporate this "obstacle" in our planning. Today, it is a beautiful focal point in the yard that was used as a backdrop for the remainder of the landscaping project.

In applying this lesson spiritually, I needed to ask how I was doing in surrendering to God the obstacles that were beyond my control and letting him use them to his glory.

> In the same way, the Spirit helps us in our weakness. We do not know what we ought to pray for, but the Spirit himself intercedes for us with groans that words cannot express. And he who searches our hearts knows the mind of the Spirit, because the Spirit intercedes for the saints in accordance with God's will.
> And we know that in all things God works for the good of those who love him, who have been called according to his purpose. (Romans 8:26–28)

Next, in order to proceed with the yard, we needed to contact our town council as we lived next to a wetlands area. Our need to add several loads of topsoil to level the land had to be approved. As with the yard, sometimes in life I can be tempted to move ahead with what I think is best without seeking advice and counsel on how my actions will affect others. Building a backyard takes research, thinking and advice. Certainly, growing spiritually takes more, not less. The stakes are not even comparable.

With approval from our town, we then had soil hauled in and planted grass. A friend installed sprinklers. From his experience we learned the importance of watering consistently, but at different times and in different amounts. We planted and we watered...and God made the grass grow.

I am reminded often of this process as I seek to grow spiritually in my life, as well as plant the seed of God's word by sharing it with others. I can't ignore what is required for nurturing and the need to be diligent in my care.

However, the miracle of a seed dying in the ground and growing always belongs to God. It is far beyond my ability to cause this to happen.

After my mom's death, some friends helped me begin a garden in her memory. She loved flowers and loved to garden. I am reminded from this of how we often desire to take on attributes of someone we love and admire. I think this is what Jesus had in mind when he asked Peter three times if Peter loved him. Hearing Peter's responses he repeatedly stated, "Feed my sheep."

Jesus' love is for his sheep (us). When I grow in love for Jesus, I take on more and more of his heart for his sheep. The things important to him become important to me.

As I learned to garden, I came to some important understandings about plants, such as zone hardiness, deer and rabbit resistance, recommended sunlight and shade times, and the timetable for blooms in order to have flowering plants throughout the season.

This cup of learning from the garden teaches me to

take the time to understand how each individual person is unique. I must make the effort to know someone. I am challenged by the apostle Paul's words in Romans 15:7:

> Accept one another, then, just as Christ accepted you, in order to bring praise to God.

As I planted my flowers, I had to learn to dig deep enough and wide enough. Too shallow a hole made the plants vulnerable to heat and one too deep kept them from getting the sun they needed. The spacing would help the scenery to be a beautiful sight when the flowers all bloomed together. Such it is when we are all blooming where we are planted. It is a glorious sight to God and to those who see it working together. Voilà! Our forest of trees had finally become a beautiful backyard.

I learned that gardening requires hard work and discomfort. It also requires getting very dirty. I learned to enjoy garden "dirt" because I knew the results would be breathtaking. I could decide that gardening would be a drudgery or a satisfying joy.

Our spiritual growth takes no less hard work, discomfort and getting dirty. Grubs, weeds and crabgrass (and other tools of Satan) are always lurking, desiring to take away from the beauty. In my physical garden I had to do continual weed clearing as I walked by, as well as occasional "bringing in the big guns" of various weed-eating tools. Continual weeding is certainly no less needed in a spiritual sense.

I also learned a valuable lesson on pruning. One day after the leaves had fallen, my husband chopped down (nearly to the roots) an unsightly "bush." He did not realize that this seemingly unsightly thing was my gorgeous, and ever so fragrant, lilac tree that overhung the deck. I cried when I saw the meager remains, sure that it was gone forever.

The lilac disaster (so I thought), turned out to be a huge blessing. Two years later, my lilac tree was loaded with phenomenal purple treasures that smelled heavenly. They were fuller and more beautiful than ever!

Sometimes I have to go beyond what is comfortable to let God and others prune my life spiritually. This can be deep like the lilac, or steady but more gentle tactics like "heading" (pinching the already bloomed tops in order to ensure continual blooming).

One of my favorite backyard stories teaches me perseverance. One cold February day after the snow had partially melted, I saw something purple on the ground. Upon closer scrutiny, I discovered it was a pansy peeking through the snow. I had planted it the previous summer, and it should not have survived the harsh winter. It was not meant to be that hardy.

However, it did survive and it thrived. I took a photo to remind me of the lessons I wanted to remember from that fragile but tough pansy (that sounds like an oxymoron). With God, we have the opportunity to keep blooming even when the circumstances are tough. Paul describes this kind of faith in 2 Corinthians 4:9 when he says "we may be knocked down but never knocked out" (Phillips Translation).

Our faith in God determines our perspective and our ability to bloom. Our faith enables us to persevere. I am reminded of an older woman who cheerfully stated to her husband after her doctor's visit, "The doctor told me I looked like a fresh, new breath of spring." After a pause, and wanting to be completely honest, she said, "He may not have said it just like that, but it's what he meant. He told me I looked like the end of a long, hard winter!"

May our faith keep our hearts like the fresh breath of spring!

> The desert and the parched land will be glad;
>   the wilderness will rejoice and blossom.
> Like the crocus, it will burst into bloom;
>   it will rejoice greatly and shout for joy.

The glory of Lebanon will be given to it,
   the splendor of Carmel and Sharon;
they will see the glory of the LORD,
   the splendor of our God. (Isaiah 35:1–2)

I love to sit in my backyard and drink my cup of learning. Thank you, God.

Thoughts from the Author

As I close my eyes I can still hear my dad's booming voice and picture his huge smile as he quotes from Luke 6:38:

> "Give, and it will be given to you. A good measure, pressed down, shaken together and running over, will be poured into your lap. For with the measure you use, it will be measured to you."

He would then state, "You can never outgive God."

I have seen this come true in my life over and over again. It has been helpful for me to reflect on the workings of God throughout my life as he is attempting to mold me and shape me into a more "noble vessel" (2 Timothy 2:21).

This past Sunday my husband inquired as to the origin of the large brown spot on the back of my shirt. I explained that before the church service began, a friend had shared her "morning cup" with me. While talking and exchanging a friendly hug, she accidentally poured her cup of coffee down my back.

As I washed out the stain, I realized that the "morning cups" so many have offered me have often left an indelible mark on my heart. I treasure these lessons. It has been a privilege to share some of them with you.

I pray to continue to hold my cup out to God. As he fills it, I know it will spill over the brim and pour into my lap (in a good way).

I pray that you will continue to let God fill your cup so it overflows to those around you now as well as to those in the next generation.

Other Writings

The following writings are chapters I wrote in several anthologies published by DPI. I offer these as added resources and encouraging helps. Note that the publication date of some of these chapters was several years ago, so some of the life facts reflect this difference.

Abigail: Living Victoriously
She Shall Be Called Woman *Volume One*

1 Samuel 25:3–42, 27:3, 30:5; 2 Samuel 2:2, 3:3;
1 Chronicles 3:1

King Saul had chosen to lead Israel his way, not God's way. It was Saul's rejection that caused God ultimately to reject him as king. He knew that God had anointed David, but that did not cause him to relinquish his throne. On the contrary, Saul chose to fight God's decision by embarking upon an obsessive mission of personal vengeance to eliminate David.

Saul turned his military forces away from fighting the enemies of Israel to pursuing his own personal enemy, David. David never fought back; he simply ran for his life. David ran to caves, to foreign cities, even to Israel's worst enemies. Along the way, he gathered hundreds of loyal volunteer followers, among them, many brave fighting men.

Although David's men would have liked to kill Saul, David never allowed it, but held valiantly to his integrity and his dependence on God's decision and intervention. While David was running for his life, narrowly escaping Saul's murderous pursuit, he and his men came to Maon. They met some shepherds there who were watching the vast flocks of a very wealthy man named Nabal.

David, the former shepherd, greatly impressed Nabal's servants by the protective and courteous treatment he gave them while he was in their neighborhood. So when David and his men had a serious need, he expected reciprocal hospitality, but Nabal rudely refused. His wife, Abigail, however, had a different heart and character.

What will I be when I grow up? Will I marry? Who will I marry? Will I have children?

These are questions pondered by young girls today as well as in the days of Abigail. A child who grew up to be an "intelligent and beautiful woman" would have had these questions (1 Samuel 25:3). She would have had the imagination to dream of betrothal to a wonderfully handsome, strong and kind man. One who would adore her and be respected at the city gate.

Yet, who materialized as this man of her dreams? Nabal, the bully. A man who was "surly and mean in his dealings" (25:3). A man of whom his servants would say, "He is such a wicked man that no one can talk with him" (25:17). Abigail was dealt a challenging life situation. Once married to this ill-tempered man, she showed a strength of character that overcame difficult circumstances instead of being overcome by them.

Adopt an Attitude

Abigail had to choose the attitude with which she would live each day. She could be miserable, full of self-pity and a discouragement to those around her. After all, she faced insensitivity day in and day out.

Or, she could choose to be bitter. *Why did God allow this to happen to me? It is his fault. I do not deserve this. And Nabal, that fool. He has ruined my life. What if I had married someone else? I would be happy then. How could any human being be so horrible? Perhaps I would feel better if I made him miserable. Punish him with the cold shoulder, sharp glances, terse words, apathy. Make him pay.*

She could live each day hoping it would be different. *He's smiling this morning. Maybe today will be different.* Yet, he never changed. Then that could have made her depressed. *I had hoped things would be different. Isn't that faith?* When her expectations let her down, she could have chosen to be cynical towards life.

Abigail had a tough situation and could have chosen any of these attitudes. Let us look at the character and actions which enabled her to overcome this difficult situation.

Opt to Overcome

Grapes were drying or being pressed into juice that was poured into skins. Sheep were hanging, being dressed for dinner. The smell of grain roasting mixed with the aroma of loaves and cakes baking. This is the backdrop in 1 Samuel 25 as Abigail is busy working and organizing the women around her.

Abigail accepted her lot in life and was making the most of it, instead of being unproductive and surrounding herself with self-pity and regret. She could have authored the phrase "God grant me the patience to accept the things I cannot change, courage to change the things I can change, and the wisdom to know the difference." There was no change on the horizon for her situation, yet she was making her life productive.

The second way Abigail overcame her difficult situation was that she took help from others. She would have remained in ignorance had she not listened to her servant who explained what Nabal had done and what David had planned. Often others can give us information, advice or scriptures that we would not know without their help. Abigail is an example of having wisdom by letting others help her.

Abigail was also a positive thinker. She overcame her tough life situation by having an attitude of "let's see how it can be done." In verse 17, the servant says to Abigail, "Now, think it over and see what you can do." There was an expectation that Abigail would do something that would make a difference.

Think about the situation. A king with four hundred men against one evil man. How tempting it would be for Abigail to resign herself to the obvious outcome, thinking she could make no difference. She believed her life *could* make a difference—even in a seemingly impossible situation. The women around Abigail caught this spirit of initiative as they quickly responded to her plan and went on ahead of her. Abigail's attitude influenced the lives of those around her. They, too, had become women of initiative, courage and faith.

Hate to Hesitate

Abigail believed that *sooner was better than later*. How often great faith, good intentions and high ideals get buried beneath mounds of procrastination. Abigail overcame her circumstances by being urgent. She "lost no time" (v18). She moved "quickly" (vv23, 33, 42). David tells Abigail in verse 23 that if she had not acted quickly he would have done great harm.

When we are dealing with people like Nabal, who are difficult and sinful, do we realize that the root of the problem is that they are in need of a Savior and a complete character change by God? Do we act quickly, like Abigail, to help them learn how to be made right with God? Or do we think that there is always more time? If Abigail had waited, it would have been too late.

Persevere with a Plan

Abigail combined initiative with personal responsibility. She took action to solve the problem. She did not wait for someone else *out there somewhere* to do it. She went to David and took the blame for her husband's behavior. This showed great humility and opened the door for mercy from David. She was willing to risk her life to help someone more undeserving. Only a humble heart, taught by the heart of God, could have done this. She did not know how David or Nabal would respond to her. Yet, she knew that following God meant personal risk. She had the courage to step out in faith in the face of great risk and the lack of support from her husband. It takes courage and persistence to go alone and keep doing good without encouragement from those close to you. But it can be done. Abigail did it. Nothing stopped Abigail. Does anything stop you?

When we are caught up in circumstances beyond our control we often become caught up in self-pity also. The best offensive against self-pity is a good plan of action. Look at what you can do, not at what you cannot do. Look out for the needs of others who need even more help than you. This is what Abigail did.

Bring Out the Best

Perhaps the most important aspect of overcoming her difficult situation was Abigail's dependence on God's truths. Though David was a powerful man, she boldly called him to the future and his accountability before God. In verses 26–31 she plead with him not to repay evil for evil. She brought the best out of David, calling upon his desire to be faithful to God's truths.

But how do we show good judgment and dependence on God as Abigail did when the pressure is on us? Do we follow Abigail's example of firmly establishing God and his standards as the priority in our lives? Do we think ahead to practical ways we can put this principle into practice? Abigail's priority led her to good judgment. Her good judgment brought the best out of someone. Poor judgment and timing can tempt even the good-hearted to do wrong in reaction. Abigail took the time to consider how to stir another up to love and good deeds (Hebrews 10:24). She was also convinced that David, striving to follow God, was full of goodness (Romans 15:14). Then she helped to draw that goodness out in him. Do we, like Abigail, bring out the best in other people?

Reap a Reward

God did not forget Abigail, and he will not forget you. Abigail was rewarded for her righteousness and courage. In the same way, if we have the same good character traits that help us overcome problems, we will be rewarded. If your husband is not a disciple, it may mean that if you persist in your example, he will become a new person in Christ. Or it may mean that you will grow in your character and become more like Christ because of overcoming a challenging circumstance. The circumstance, like Nabal, might never change, but if we continue to do good and grow in God's grace by the power of God, one day we will hear, "Well done, good and faithful servant! Come and share your master's happiness" (Matthew 25:21).

Never Give In or Give Up

I am an idealist at heart. I like everything to turn out "happily ever after." I want to know that the movie will end okay before I pay money to watch it.

Yet, time and time again, I see injustices in life. Some are physical and some are situational. Yet I know that God loves each person individually and that every injustice in life brings the opportunity for the light to shine and for God to be glorified. I have known that for a long time, and yet I remember well a particular *Nabal* in my life whom I allowed to cause me to lose faith and become bitter and cynical.

My husband and I had not been in the ministry long and were seeing God work powerfully in many people's lives. We were in a small traditional type of church. I assumed that everyone in the church, especially the leaders, would want to see the church grow and would pour their lives into that task. We worked hard, my husband preached the Word, and we gave our hearts to the people.

What a shock it was to discover one day that a leader in this church was standing in the back as people left, handing out material full of lies and prejudices against us. My faith waned, my anger grew, and I stewed inside. Why did this happen? We were trying our hardest only to be "slam dunked." Hatred started to grow in my heart. Cynicism started creeping in, and I became somewhat aloof and apathetic. My husband had been hurt. I had been hurt, and it was not fair.

I had to wrestle in my heart with the things I was feeling. I watched my husband respond with honesty, but not bitterness. He had decided to respond righteously. I read the Scriptures and hung on to the ones about the kingdom of God and God's faithfulness, even when people are faithless. I thought about Jesus on the cross and his incredible forgiveness and wondered if I could do that.

As I think about Abigail I realize how close I came to living a life of bitterness, retaliation and cynicism when confronted with a *Nabal* in my life. Her life inspires me to see unfair situations in a different light. I have seen many *Nabals* in my life and others' lives since that time. I am determined to be like Abigail and trust God and never give in or give up.

I have already experienced great rewards. I have the privilege of seeing the kingdom of God that I read about in the Bible lived out in flesh and blood. I see unity forged, and I look forward to an eternity with my Father in heaven.

Focus question:

When you are tested by a difficult situation in your life, do you act righteously and quickly?

Speaking the Truth in Love
Glory in the Church

Then we will no longer be infants, tossed back and
forth by the waves, and blown here and there by
every wind of teaching and by the cunning and
craftiness of men in their deceitful scheming. Instead,
speaking the truth in love, we will in all things grow up
into him who is the Head, that is, Christ.

Ephesians 4:14–15

This chapter is for all conflict avoiders. I had to laugh when I received this topic because speaking the truth has been so hard for me. Conflict avoidance runs deep in my sinful nature. Sinful…because it is a sin not to speak the truth in order to avoid conflict. At this point in my life, though it is often difficult, God is making me strong where I am weak.

I can remember an instance in kindergarten when I ran away from school and hid in my garage rather than tell my teacher that I had forgotten my lunch money! Later in life, my college roommate was designated "Martyr of the Month" in my dorm because I had spoken the truth to her about God. I had come a long way from hiding in the garage.

After I was married and was serving full-time in the ministry, I gently shared with an older woman what I believed the younger women in the congregation needed her to be as a role model. The next thing I knew, she was upset, her husband was upset and my husband was fired.

Then, somewhere along the way, I lost my conviction and courage, and instead of speaking the truth in love, I started stuffing the truth in fear.

Stuffing the Truth in Fear

Jesus is truth. He was known, even as the Pharisees tried to trap him in his words, as a man of integrity and a man of truth. "Teacher, we know you are a man of integrity. You aren't swayed by men, because you pay no attention to who they are; but you teach the way of God in accordance with the truth" (Mark 12:14).

Jesus was a man of deep conviction. His convictions were based on God's truth, not on other people's opinions. How often do we stuff the truth because we are afraid of what people will think of us or how they will react? I feared people's reactions so much that I learned a common stuffing technique. I would subconsciously reason that *I should not* feel or think a certain thing so therefore *I would not.* I learned to deny feelings rather than be open with them.

Speak the Truth to Everyone

Speaking the truth in love applies to all of our life situations. First, we must learn to speak the truth to ourselves. Sometimes, we deny what we really think, even in our own hearts and minds. We can also react defensively to others, to the Bible or to a sermon. Insecurity and pride often keep us from welcoming the truth into our hearts. Do you make it easy for others to speak the truth to you?

Second, we must speak the truth to our brothers and sisters. Unresolved attitudes bring about deceit, bitterness and slander. When we have quiet reservations about someone's motives and assume the worst, Satan wins. Jesus loved his friends enough to bring things into the light. He went beyond the shallow conversation and into the attitudes of the heart. "What were you arguing about on the road?" Jesus asked his disciples in Mark 9:33. He set us an example in being direct and speaking to the heart.

Third, we must love the lost enough to speak the truth to them. Jesus spoke to a man who "had it all" in Mark 10. Verse 21 simply states, "Jesus looked at him and loved him." He proved his love by speaking the truth about how the man could inherit eternal life. Do we see others through Jesus' eyes of compassion? No matter what is on the outside, without spiritual truth we are all helpless and harassed, like sheep without a shepherd.

Love Is a Safe Place

In order to "speak the truth in love," it helps to know that "in love" is a safe place. I found it hard to be vulnerable until I learned that the unconditional love in the kingdom of God is a safe place. There was a time in my life when I had a lot of hurt feelings and attitudes toward another disciple. I didn't want to have these feelings, so I pretended I didn't. I was afraid to express them honestly. A brother asked me if I believed I was in a safe place in the kingdom of God. The tears flowed as I saw the beauty of God's plan. I spoke the truth and the sister and I ended up closer than ever.

Speaking the truth in love is always for the purpose of building up. Perhaps much of the fear often associated with speaking the truth would be alleviated if we made a daily effort to encourage one another on the truth about the good things. This, too, is a significant part of speaking the truth in love. It does not only mean talking about conflict and hard teachings. The truth also consists of whatever is noble, right, pure, lovely, admirable, excellent or praiseworthy (Philippians 4:8).

Time to Grow Up

Conviction about God's word, planted deep in our hearts and flowing freely from our mouths, is the means by which we grow from infants into grown-ups. If we stuff the truth in fear, we will vacillate between what everyone else thinks and what we know is true; and we will know in our heart of hearts that we are being cowards.

However, when we hold firmly to the truth, and love God and others enough to express it, "we will no longer be infants, tossed back and forth by the waves.... Instead, speaking the truth in love, we will in all things grow up into him who is the Head, that is, Christ" (Ephesians 4:14–15).

Not Surprised by Joy
Thirty Days at the Foot of the Cross

Let us fix our eyes on Jesus, the author and perfecter of our faith, who for the joy set before him endured the cross, scorning its shame, and sat down at the right hand of the throne of God. Consider him who endured such opposition from sinful men, so that you will not grow weary and lose heart,

Hebrews 12:2–3

Jesus was a joyful person. But joy at the foot of the cross? It seems rather improbable. How can you be joyful when circumstances seem to be deteriorating right before your eyes? When health and prosperity abound and when family and friends are treating you well, it's not so hard to be happy. But when times are tough, joy can seem elusive.

As we go to the foot of the cross and fix our eyes on Jesus, we understand the secret of true joy. On the cross Jesus was rejected by many "friends." Instead of health he experienced suffering and death. As for prosperity, lots were cast for the shirt on his back. In fact, at the cross it seemed that everything was going wrong. Jesus was being mocked and murdered. His life was ending not in glory, but in shame. No "leagues of angels" came down to save the day. Yet joy was still in the heart of Jesus because he knew that God was in control and that his life would somehow bring glory to God and hope to us. He didn't argue with God. He didn't need to explain it all as he said his last few words. He didn't need to defend or justify himself to the crowd for the terrible injustices he had received. The Scriptures say that he entrusted himself to the one who judges justly (1 Peter 2:23).

When we try to take over God's role and insist on having everything figured out, we end up putting *him* on trial and standing in judgment of God himself. There is no joy in that posture.

For Jesus, there was a joy-producing freedom and peace in his acceptance of God's plan and protection. He knew he would have eternal fellowship with his Father in heaven and that all the trouble and pain we experience is not even worth comparing to what God has prepared for us (2 Corinthians 4:17).

Throughout the last days of Jesus' life on earth, he prayed for his disciples to have the full measure of his joy (John 17:13). Jesus was a joyful person. Jesus was able to look beyond the day's circumstances with an eternal and hopeful perspective. He trusted his Father.

What does this mean for you and me? When we don't understand circumstances happening around us, do we trust God, really? Or do we constantly question and sit in judgment of him? I've never met a truly happy person who tried to stand in God's place. Such a person becomes bitter and cynical. We cannot find joy trying to be something we were never meant to be.

Do you understand that Jesus is aware of and cares about your situation? He is able to work all things together for good. Even the violent scene of the cross brought about our hope and salvation. Do you understand that Jesus is preparing an eternal place for you where there is no sorrow or pain?

When I trust the fact that God is in control of my life and that he does not "mess up" in his plan for me, I do have a joyful perspective on life. When I do not trust God, I become anxious and critical.

One of our daughters has an illness that has caused her to be sick for many days over a two-year period. When either of us is tempted to blame God or to feel sorry for ourselves, we lose our joy and settle into depression. This trial has not been pleasant to undergo, but I know God is strengthening her character and will use all things to his glory. She has learned to be thankful for God's many blessings—on the sick days and the well days.

Thankfulness springs from a trusting heart and gives birth to joy. You choose how you will fill your heart and mind. You can choose to be a thankful person or you can choose to keep a mental and verbal list of all the people and things you don't like. When I feel depleted of joy, I decide to be thankful to God, praying a prayer of thanksgiving until I'm happy. When I focus on being thankful, happiness is not far behind. Ask God to fill you with joy. Joy is a fruit of the Spirit, and he longs to fill you with it as you trust in him (Romans 15:13).

The joy of Jesus' relationship with God and the joy of his mission for others enabled him to endure the cross. He pushed through the cross, trusting God and knowing that our salvation was on the other side. Isaiah 53:11 says "After the suffering of his soul, he will see the light of life and be satisfied."

Even the cross did not keep Jesus from being joyful. What will you allow to steal your joy? Are you rationalizing? Excusing your lack of joy? Blaming it on circumstances in your life? Fix your eyes on Jesus. He will teach you to trust and to be thankful, and in so doing, to find true joy. May you, too, see the light of life.

✳

For further study:
Job 6:10
Psalm 5:11
19:8, 28:7, 51:12
John 15:11, 16:20–22, 17:13

Romans 14:17
2 Corinthians 8:2
1 Thessalonians 1:6
James 1:2

Changes in Character
Teach Us to Pray

Surely you desire truth in the inner parts;
  you teach me wisdom in the inmost place.

Psalm 51:6

As I write this article, I look at a piece of torn, battered paper that is like an old friend to me. It is a page from my prayer list that I have prayed through over and over again. I purposely did not type it up to look fancy because I wanted its simplicity to remind me that before God, my character is exposed. I must look at the inner parts, the inmost places.

Clearly Defined

There are other pages to my prayer list that remind me of people and situations that need my prayers. No prayer is easy, but when I get to this page I must take a sober, gut-level look at who I am before God. It is a page entitled "character." Here I pray through the things in my character that need to change from weaknesses into strengths. As I pray through these things, I am reminded of the words in the song "Jesus Loves Me": "I am weak, but he is strong." Praying through them day after day forces me to rely on God and strengthens my faith as I have seen him answer my prayers time and time again.

Too often we stay generic in our prayers: "Help me be a better person, help me to change, to love you more, God…"

Too often we don't know what specifically we need to change and so don't have a clear aim in going after it. When we aim at nothing, that is what we get. Can you put your character sins and weaknesses into words? Are they clearly defined in your mind? If they are not, it is unlikely you will be victorious in overcoming them.

In Touch with the Truth

We learn the truth about our character from the word of God which discerns the thoughts and intentions of our heart (Hebrews 4:12–13) and is a mirror reflecting what we look like spiritually (James 1:23–25).

We also learn the truth about ourselves from other people in our lives (Proverbs 20:5). I remember years ago when I was a freshman in college and was given many new responsibilities of leadership. I was ambitious—part righteous, part selfish. I would read Philippians 2:3: "Do nothing out of selfish ambition," and see selfish thoughts in my heart hoping to "get credit for good deeds." I hated this in my heart and it dogged my feet. I remember crying out to God again and again, confessing to God what was there and begging him to take it away. I thought it would never leave me, but I took comfort in the scripture, "Resist the devil, and he will flee from you" (James 4:7). Finally, my character began to really change.

Several years ago I learned, through a relationship, how much deceit was in my character. I would stuff things I felt instead of saying what was in my heart. I could make something seem or sound better in my mind or with someone else. Openness and persistence in prayer, and openness with other people has allowed my conscience to become very alert and tender in this area, so that I am able to change.

Partner to deceit in my character is fear. Fear of conflict, fear of being vulnerable in my weakness, fear of God being against me, fear of heights, fear of fear…. When someone shared with me one day that they didn't think I was a very "open" person, it bothered me deeply, but I did not "get it." I didn't know how to change. I cried to God; I begged him to change me. I asked him to help me see it. I fasted; I went out to a quiet place for a day of prayer. Finally, I got it. I saw the fear and deceit and begged God to take it. I would talk about it with others and ask them how I was doing at being open and vulnerable. Today God has turned that weakness into a strength.

Keep Growing

Ask God to help you see what you need to change. Ask others what things they see in your sinful nature, those deep-rooted things that don't go easily. What are they for you? Self-pity? Arrogance (self-reliance)? Timidity? A weak will? Bitterness? Being quick to quit? Lacking passion and fire for God? Lack of discipline? Maybe you have trouble getting on an emotional heart level with people or struggle with respecting your husband.

There are things I include like being on time, being more emotionally expressive to my husband and verbally appreciative for my friends. At times when I have felt stuck and lacked motivation, I have followed Philippians 2:13: "for it is God who works in you to will and to act…." I make myself stay and pray for the "want to" as well as the power. God has always been faithful. At times I've fasted and prayed or driven to my "special prayer places." I know several sisters who recently stayed up all night praying to change something in their character.

How badly do you want to change? It will show by the way you pray. Many times when I pray about changing my character, I remind God (though I know he hasn't forgotten) of his promise in 2 Corinthians 12:9: "My power is made perfect in weakness." I picture in my mind's eye the weakness being a strength and how that would show itself practically in my life. That thought fires me up and gives me my goal. God, with all his unlimited means, will get me there. I can't quit until I'm there, or when I get there.

Prayer

My great and wonderful God and Father, I stand in awe as I think of the magnificent ways you have brought about change since the beginning. When all was void you spoke the world into existence. You changed a particle of dust into a human form and with your breath changed this form into man, made in your image. From his rib you fashioned a woman and from this couple, a child.

You changed an ocean into dry land, water into wine, five loaves and two fish into a feast that fed a multitude. You changed death into resurrection and eternal life. You changed timid, uneducated people into powerful, bold disciples, and persecutors into church leaders.

More recently Father, I have seen your hand at work in the winds of change. You have taken down the Iron Curtain, dismantled the Berlin Wall and undone South African apartheid. When you are in the picture, God, things change.

When I think of all your awesome deeds and realize how faithless I can be when it comes to changing me, I am ashamed. Forgive me. I want to love like you love, care like you care, get disturbed when you are disturbed…to be like you more each day. I want to set the standard for my character that you have set in your Word.

God, help me to see the things I need to change and to have the humility, courage and perseverance to change. Turn my weaknesses into strengths so that my life can display the glory of your power and more people can come to know you.

Father, though you are the author of true change, thank you that you remain the same perfect, powerful and loving God yesterday, today and forever. I do believe that you can turn my weaknesses into strengths. Thank you so much. I love you with all of my heart.

Love, Jeanie

❉

For further study:

2 Corinthians 3:17–18
2 Peter 1:3–8
Philippians 2:12–13

Books for Christian Growth from Illumination Publishers

Apologetics

Compelling Evidence for God and the Bible—Truth in an Age of Doubt, by Douglas Jacoby.
Field Manual for Christian Apologetics, by John M. Oakes.
Is There A God—Questions and Answers about Science and the Bible, by John M. Oakes.
Mormonism—What Do the Evidence and Testimony Reveal?, by John M. Oakes.
Reasons For Belief-A Handbook of Christian Evidence, by John M. Oakes.
That You May Believe—Reflections on Science and Jesus, by John Oakes/David Eastman.
The Resurrection: A Historical Analysis, by C. Foster Stanback.
When God Is Silent—The Problem of Human Suffering, by Douglas Jacoby.

Bible Basics

A Disciple's Handbook—Third Edition, Tom A. Jones, Editor.
A Quick Overview of the Bible, by Douglas Jacoby.
Be Still, My Soul—A Practical Guide to a Deeper Relationship with God, by Sam Laing.
From Shadow to Reality—Relationship of the Old & New Testament, by John M. Oakes.
Getting the Most from the Bible, Second Edition, by G. Steve Kinnard.
Letters to New Disciples—Practical Advice for New Followers of Jesus, by Tom A. Jones.
The Baptized Life—The Lifelong Meaning of Immersion into Christ, by Tom A. Jones.
The Lion Never Sleeps—Preparing Those You Love for Satans Attacks, by Mike Taliaferro.
The New Christian's Field Guide, Joseph Dindinger, Editor.
Thirty Days at the Foot of the Cross, Tom and Sheila Jones, Editors.

Christian Living

But What About Your Anger—A Biblical Guide to Managing Your Anger, by Lee Boger.
Caring Beyond the Margins—Understanding Homosexuality, by Guy Hammond.
Golden Rule Membership—What God Expects of Every Disciple, by John M. Oakes.
How to Defeat Temptation in Under 60 Seconds, by Guy Hammond.
Jesus and the Poor—Embracing the Ministry of Jesus, by G. Steve Kinnard.
How to Be a Missionary in Your Hometown, by Joel Nagel.
Like a Tree Planted by Streams of Water—Personal Spiritual Growth, G. Steve Kinnard.
Love One Another—Importance & Power of Christian Relationships, by Gordon Ferguson.
One Another—Transformational Relationships, by Tom A. Jones and Steve Brown.
Prepared to Answer—Restoring Truth in An Age of Relativism, by Gordon Ferguson.
Repentance—A Cosmic Shift of Mind & Heart, by Edward J. Anton.
Strong in the Grace—Reclaiming the Heart of the Gospel, by Tom A. Jones.
The Guilty Soul's Guide to Grace—Freedom in Christ, by Sam Laing.
The Power of Discipling, by Gordon Ferguson.
The Prideful Soul's Guide to Humility, by Tom A. Jones and Michael Fontenot.
The Way of the Heart—Spiritual Living in a Legalistic World, by G. Steve Kinnard.
The Way of the Heart of Jesus—Prayer, Fasting, Bible Study, by G. Steve Kinnard.
Till the Nets Are Full—An Evangelism Handbook for the 21st Century, by Douglas Jacoby.
Walking the Way of the Heart—Lessons for Spiritual Living, by G. Steve Kinnard.
Values and Habits of Spiritual Growth, by Bryan Gray.

Deeper Study

A Women's Ministry Handbook, by Jennifer Lambert and Kay McKean.

After The Storm—Hope & Healing From Ezra—Nehemiah, by Rolan Dia Monje.

Aliens and Strangers—The Life and Letters of Peter, by Brett Kreider.

Crossing the Line: Culture, Race, and Kingdom, by Michael Burns.

Daniel—Prophet to the Nations, by John M. Oakes.

Exodus—Making Israel's Journey Your Own, by Rolan Dia Monje.

Exodus—Night of Redemption, by Douglas Jacoby.

Finish Strong—The Message of Haggai, Zechariah, and Malachi, by Rolan Dia Monje.

In Remembrance of Me—Understanding the Lord's Supper, by Andrew C. Fleming.

In the Middle of It!—Tools to Help Preteen and Young Teens, by Jeff Rorabaugh.

Into the Psalms—Verses for the Heart, Music for the Soul, by Rolan Dia Monje.

King Jesus—A Survey of the Life of Jesus the Messiah, by G. Steve Kinnard.

Jesus Unequaled—An Exposition of Colossians, by G. Steve Kinnard.

Passport to the Land of Enough—Revised Edition, by Joel Nagel.

Prophets I—The Voices of Yahweh, by G. Steve Kinnard

Prophets II—The Prophets of the Assyrian Period, by G. Steve Kinnard

Prophets III—The Prophets of the Babylonian and Persion Periods, by G. Steve Kinnard.

Return to Sender—When There's Nowhere Left to God but Home, by Guy Hammond.

Romans—The Heart Set Free, by Gordon Ferguson.

Revelation Revealed—Keys to Unlocking the Mysteries of Revelation, by Gordon Ferguson.

Spiritual Leadership for Women, Jeanie Shaw, Editor.

The Call of the Wise—An Introduction and Index of Proverbs, by G. Steve Kinnard.

*The Cross of the Savior—From the Perspective of Jesus...by Mark Templer.

The Final Act—A Biblical Look at End-Time Prophecy, by G. Steve Kinnard.

The Gospel of Matthew—The Crowning of the King, by G. Steve Kinnard.

The Letters of James, Peter, John, Jude—Life to the Full, by Douglas Jacoby.

The Lion Has Roared—An Exposition of Amos, by Douglas Jacoby.

The Seven People Who Help You to Heaven, by Sam Laing.

The Spirit—Presense & Power, Sense & Nonsense, by Douglas Jacoby.

Thrive—Using Psalms to Help You Flourish, by Douglas Jacoby.

What Happens After We Die?, by Dr. Douglas Jacoby.

World Changers—The History of the Church in the Book of Acts, by Gordon Ferguson.

Marriage and Family

Building Emotional Intimacy in Your Marriage, by Jeff and Florence Schachinger.

Hot and Holy—God's Plan for Exciting Sexual Intimacy in Marriage, by Sam Laing.

Friends & Lovers—Marriage as God Designed It, by Sam and Geri Laing.

Mighty Man of God—A Return to the Glory of Manhood, by Sam Laing.

Raising Awesome Kids—Being the Great Influence in Your Kids' Lives by Sam and Geri Laing.

Principle-Centered Parenting, by Douglas and Vicki Jacoby.

The Essential 8 Principles of a Growing Christian Marriage, by Sam and Geri Laing.

The Essential 8 Principles of a Strong Family, by Sam and Geri Laing.

Warrior—A Call to Every Man Everywhere, by Sam Laing.

All these and more available at www.ipibooks.com

www.ipibooks.com